Whitefield's Sermon Outlines

THE WORLD'S GREAT SERMONS IN OUTLINE

Selected and Edited by
SHELDON B. QUINCER

VOLUME I
Alexander Maclaren's Sermon Outlines

VOLUME II
Matthew Henry's Sermon Outlines

VOLUME III
George Whitefield's Sermon Outlines

VOLUME IV
Joseph Parker's Sermon Outlines

VOLUME V
Jonathan Edwards' Sermon Outlines

The World's Great Sermons in Outline

Whitefield's
SERMON OUTLINES

A CHOICE COLLECTION OF THIRTY-FIVE MODEL SERMONS

by

GEORGE WHITEFIELD

Selected and Edited by

SHELDON B. QUINCER, D.D.
Baptist Theological Seminary
Grand Rapids, Michigan

WM. B. EERDMANS PUBLISHING CO.
Grand Rapids, Michigan

Foreword

One of the greatest revivals of American history was the Great Awakening of the eighteenth century. The beginning of the century saw most of our churches cold and lifeless. A few godly men saw the desperate conditions and were used of God in starting revival fires, but it was not until the arrival of English born George Whitefield in 1740 that the fires were flamed into a blaze that swept the eastern seaboard and Georgia. Under God, Whitefield became the leader of the revival.

He belonged to all denominations — he was ordained as an Anglican, became a Calvinistic Methodist, and was buried under the pulpit of the Federal Street Presbyterian Church of Newburyport, Mass. He preached wherever he had the opportunity, in church buildings regardless of denominational affiliation, and in the open fields.

In thirty-five wears of Gospel ministry in the British Isles, West Indies, and America, Whitefield preached 18,000 sermons to audiences which sometimes numbered 30,000 people.

His sermons are both doctrinal and practical. In reading them one is impressed with his emphasis on the total depravity of man, the righteousness of Christ, and the grace of God. To him man is a sinner in need of Christ's imputed righteousness, which he can receive only through God's grace. He firmly held that "salvation is of the Lord."

Born in his father's tavern in Gloucester in December 1714, Whitefield entered Oxford University at the age of 18 and three years later was converted and soon thereafter began his public ministry of preaching. He died in Newburyport on September 30, 1770.

The editor wishes to acknowledge his indebtedness to the Evangelical Library of London for the loan of several volumes of Whitefield's Sermons which have been long out of print.

SHELDON B. QUINCER

Grand Rapids, Michigan
January, 1956.

Contents

Whitefield's Sermon Outlines

1

The First Promise

> *And I will put enmity between thee and the woman, and between thy seed and her seed; it shall bruise thy head, and thou shalt bruise his heel.* — Genesis 3:15

U PON CALLING your attention to the words of the text, I may address you in the language of the holy angels to the shepherds that were watching their flocks by night: "Behold, I bring you glad tidings of great joy." This is the first promise that was made of a Savior to the apostate race of Adam. It is wonderful to observe how gradually God revealed His Son to mankind. He began with the promise in the text and this the godly lived upon until the time of Abraham. To him, God made further discoveries of His eternal council concerning man's redemption. Afterwards at various times and in different ways God spoke to the fathers by the prophets until at length the Lord Jesus was manifested in flesh and came and tabernacled among us.

I. THE NEED FOR THE PROMISE.

A. The Reality of the Fall.

1. *Temptation.* In what odious colors God is here represented: "God doth know that in the day ye eat thereof, ye shall be as gods (equal with God)." Thus the grand temptation was that Adam and Eve should be hereafter under no control; equal, if not superior, to God.

2. *Sin.* Eve "took of the fruit and did eat and gave also unto her husband." What a complication of crimes in this one act of sin! Here is disbelief of God's threatening, ingratitude

11

to their Maker, and neglect of their posterity who would stand or fall with them. Never again was a crime of such a complicated nature committed by any one upon earth. Only the devil's apostasy and rebellion could equal it.

B. Realization of the Fall.

The fall of man is written in too legible characters not to be understood. Those who deny it, by their denial prove it. The heathen confess and bewail it. They can see the streams of corruption running through the whole race of mankind, but cannot trace them to the fountainhead. Before God gave a revelation of His Son, man was a riddle to himself. Moses unfolds more in this one chapter, out of which the text is taken, than all mankind could have been capable of finding out of themselves, though they had studied to all eternity.

II. THE MEANING OF THE PROMISE.

A. The Seed of the Serpent.

By the serpent's seed we are to understand the devil and all of his children who are permitted by God to tempt and to sift His children. The Lord Jesus, the seed of the woman, bruised Satan's accursed head through His suffering and death upon the cross. By dying, Christ overcame him who had the power of death, that is the devil. He thereby spoiled principalities and powers, and made a show of them openly, triumphing over them upon the cross.

B. The Seed of the Woman.

By the seed of the woman we are to understand the Lord Jesus Christ, who though God of very God, was for us men and our salvation to have a body prepared for Him by the Holy Spirit and to be born of a woman, and by His obedience and death make an atonement for man's transgression and bring in an everlasting righteousness, work in them a new nature and thereby bruise the serpent's head, that is, destroy his power and dominion over them. Satan bruised His heel when he tempted Him for forty days in the wilderness; when he raised up strong persecution against Him during His public ministry; especially when our Lord sweat great drops of blood in the Garden; when he put it in Judas' heart to destroy Him; most of all when Satan's emissaries nailed Him to the accursed tree.

III. THE FULFILLMENT OF THE PROMISE.

A. By Way of Interpretation.

This promise was literally fulfilled in the person of our Lord Jesus Christ. As we have already seen the promise refers to the Seed of the woman, Christ, and His victory on the cross over Satan; and to the seed of the Serpent, Satan and His emissaries, and their defeat at Calvary.

B. By Way of Application.

1. *This promise has been fulfilled in the children of God considered collectively.* In this promise there is an eternal enmity put between the seed of the woman and the seed of the serpent. Therefore, those that are born after the flesh cannot but persecute those who are born after the Spirit. This enmity showed itself in Cain's persecution of Abel. It continued throughout all the ages before Christ's incarnation as seen in Bible history. It raged after Christ's ascension, as witnessed by the Book of Acts and the history of the early Christians. It now rages and will continue to rage in a greater or less degree to the end of time.

2. *This promise has been fulfilled in the children of God considered individually.* In every believer there are two seeds, the seed of the woman and the seed of the serpent — the flesh lusting against the Spirit and the Spirit against the flesh. It is with the believer, when quickened with grace in his heart, as it was with Rebekah when she conceived Esau and Jacob in her womb; she felt a struggling. Thus grace and nature struggle, if I may so speak, in the womb of a believer's heart; but grace in the end shall get the better of nature. The promise in the text insures the perseverance and victory of believers.

CONCLUSION

I know in whom I have believed; I am persuaded He will keep that safe which I have committed unto Him. He is faithful who has promised that the seed of the woman shall bruise the serpent's head. May we all experience a daily completion of His promise, both in the church and in our hearts, until we come to the church of the first-born, the spirits of just men made perfect, in the presence and actual fruition of the great God our heavenly Father. To whom, with the Son and the Holy Spirit, be ascribed all honor, power, might, majesty, and dominion now and forever more. Amen.

2

Walking with God

*And Enoch walked with God; and he was
not, for God took him.* — **Genesis 5:24**

Eɴᴏᴄʜ is spoken of in the words of the text in a very
extra-ordinary manner. We have here a short but full and glorious account of his behavior in this world and the triumphant
manner of his entry into the next. The former is contained in the
words, "And Enoch walked with God." The latter in the words,
"and he was not, for God took him."

I. THE IMPLICATIONS OF WALKING WITH GOD.

A. Enmity Has Been Taken Away.

Walking with God implies that the prevailing power of the
enmity of a person's heart is taken away by the Spirit of God.
The carnal mind is enmity, not only an enemy, but enmity
itself, against God. All who know this will acknowledge walking with God requires the destruction of the power of this
heart enmity.

B. Reconciliation Has Been Effected.

Walking with God also implies that a person is actually recon-
ciled to God the Father in and through the all-sufficient
righteousness and atonement of His Son. When we are justified by faith in Christ, then, but not until then, we have peace
with God; and consequently it cannot be said until then that
we walk with Him.

C. Fellowship Is Experienced.

"And Enoch walked with God," that is, he maintained a holy, settled, habitual, although undoubtedly not altogether uninterrupted fellowship with God, in and through Jesus Christ. This walking with God consists in an habitual bent of the will for God, in an habitual dependence upon His power and promise, in an habitual voluntary dedication of our all to His glory.

D. Progress in the Christian Life.

The first idea of the word walking seems to suppose progressive motion. A person that walks, though it be more slowly, yet he goes forward and does not continue in one place. So it is with those that walk with God. They go on, as the Psalmist says, "from strength to strength" (Psalm 84:7). Read also II Corinthians 3:18 and II Peter 3:18.

II. THE MEANS OF THE MAINTENANCE OF WALKING WITH GOD.

A. Bible Reading.

Believers maintain their walk with God by reading His Holy Word. "Search the Scriptures," says our Lord, "for these are they that testify of Me" (John 5:39). The Word of God is profitable for reproof, for correction, and for instruction in righteousness, and in every way sufficient to make every true child of God thoroughly furnished unto every good work (II Timothy 3:16-17).

B. Secret Prayer.

A neglect of secret prayer has been frequently an inlet to many spiritual diseases and has been attended with fatal consequences. "Watch and pray that ye enter not into temptation" (Matthew 26:41). If you would keep up your walk with God, pray. When you are about the common business of life, be much in ejaculatory prayer. It will reach the heart of God.

C. Meditation.

Holy and frequent meditation is another blessed means of keeping up a believer's walk with God. "Prayer, reading, temptation, and meditation," says Luther, "make a minister." They also make a perfect Christian. Meditation to the soul is the same as digestion to the body. David found it so and therefore he was frequently employed in meditation, even in the night season.

D. Consideration of God's Providential Dealings.

If we believe the Scriptures we must believe our Lord's words that the hairs of our heads are numbered and the sparrow does not fall without our heavenly Father's knowledge (Matthew 10:29-30). Therefore, if believers would keep up their walk with God they must hear what the Lord has to say concerning them in the voice of His providence.

E. Consideration of the Holy Spirit's Work in the Life.

In order to walk closely with God, His children must watch the workings of His Spirit in their hearts. They must give up themselves to be guided by the Holy Spirit as a little child gives his hand to be led by the parent. It is every Christian's duty to be guided by the Spirit in conjunction with God's written Word.

F. Faithfulness to God.

It is recorded of Zacharias and Elizabeth that they walked in all God's ordinances, as well as commandments, blameless (Luke 1:6). All rightly informed Christians will look upon ordinances as their hightest privileges. They will delight to visit the place where God's honor dwelleth and to embrace all opportunities to show forth the Lord's death till He come.

G. Association with the Godly.

If you would walk with God you will associate and keep company with those that walk with Him. The early Christians, no doubt, kept up their vigor and first love by continuing in fellowship one with another. If we look into church history or observe our own times we shall find that as God's power prevails, Christian societies and fellowship meetings prevail.

III. THE MOTIVES FOR WALKING WITH GOD.

A. It Is a Walk that Is Honorable.

Do you consider it a small think to have the secret of the Lord of lords with you and to be called the friends of God? Such honor have all God's saints. "The secret of the Lord is with them that fear Him" (Psalm 25:14). "Henceforth, I call you not servants, but friends; for the servant knoweth not the will of His master" (John 15:15).

B. It Is a Walk that Is Pleasant.

The wisest of men has told us that "wisdom's ways are ways of pleasantness, and all her paths are peace" (Proverbs 3:17). And I remember Matthew Henry, when he was just about to expire, said to a friend, "You have heard many men's dying words, and these are mine: A life spent in communion with God is the most pleasant life in the world."

C. It Is a Walk which Ends in Heaven.

There is a heaven at the end of this walk. For, to use the words of Bishop Beveridge, "Though the way be narrow, yet it is not long; and though the gate be strait, yet it opens into everlasting life." Enoch found it so. He walked with God on earth and God took him to sit down with Him forever in the kingdom of heaven.

CONCLUSION

What more can I say to you that are yet strangers to Christ to come and walk with God Put on the Lord Jesus and make no longer provision for the flesh, to fulfil the lust thereof. The blood, even the precious blood of Jesus Christ, if you come to the Father in and through Him, will cleanse you from all sin.

3

The Testing of Abraham

And He said, Lay not thine hand upon the lad, neither do thou anything to him; for now I know that thou fearest God, seeing thou hast not withheld thy son, thine only son, from Me.
—Genesis 22:12

THE APOSTLE PAUL informs us that "whatsoever things were written aforetime were written for our learning, that we through patience and comfort of the Scriptures might have hope" (Romans 15:4). And as without faith it is impossible to please God or be accepted in the Son of His love; we may be assured that whatever instances of a more than common faith are recorded in the Bible, they were designed by God's Spirit for our learning and imitation. (Read Genesis 22:1-14.)

I. ABRAHAM'S TEMPTATION — verses 1-2.

A. The Time of the Temptation.

The sacred penman begins the narrative thus: "And it came to pass, after these things, God did tempt Abraham." After these things, that is, after he had undergone many severe trials, after he was old and full of days, and might flatter himself that the troubles and toils of life were now finished. Christians, you know not what trials you may meet before you die. Our last trials, in all probability, will be the greatest. We can never say our trials are finished until we leave this earthly scene.

B. The Meaning of Temptation.

Does not James tell us that God tempts no man (1:13) God tempts no man to evil. However, God may be said to tempt, I mean, to try His servants. In this sense we are to understand the passage where we are told that Jesus was "led up of the the Spirit into the wilderness to be tempted of the devil" (Matthew 4:1). In this sense we are to understand the expression before us: "God did tempt (or try) Abraham."

C. The Nature of the Temptation.

It must not only be a son, but "thine only son Isaac, whom thou lovest" (verse 2). It must be his only son, the heir of all, the son of his old age in whom his soul delighted, in whose life his own was wrapped up. This son, this only son, this Isaac, the son of his love, must be taken now and be offered up by his own father for a burnt offering upon one of the mountains of which God would tell him.

II. ABRAHAM'S RESPONSE TO THE TEMPTATION
verses 3-10.

A. It Was a Response Without Consultation with Man.

The humility, as well as the piety of the Patriarch is observable: he saddled his own beast of burden. To show his sincerity, although he took two of his young men and his son Isaac with him, yet he kept his design a secret from them all. He does not so much as tell Sarah his wife. She might hinder him in his obedience to God. The young men, had they known of it, might have forced him away from obeying God's command.

B. It Was a Response of Obedience.

"They came to the place which God had told him of; and Abraham built an altar there, and laid the wood in order, and bound Isaac his son, and laid him upon the altar upon the wood" (verse 9). Here let us pause for awhile and by faith take a view of the place where the father has laid his son. And now the fatal blow is to be given, "And Abraham stretched forth his hand, and took the knife to slay his son" (verse 10).

C. It Was a Response of Faith.

"And Abraham said, My son, God will provide Himself a lamb for a burnt offering" (verse 8). Some think that Abraham by faith saw the Lord Jesus afar off and here spoke prophetically of the Lamb of God already slain in decree and hereafter to be actually offered up for sinners. This was a Lamb of God's providing, indeed, to satisfy His own justice and to render Him just in justifying the ungodly.

III. ABRAHAM'S OBEDIENCE REWARDED
verses 11-14.

A. The Call of the Angel of the Lord.

Sing, O heavens and rejoice, O earth! Just as the knife in all probability was near Isaac's throat, "the angel of the Lord (or rather the Lord of angels, Jesus Christ, the Angel of the everlasting covenant) called unto him (probably in an audible manner) from heaven, and said, Abraham, Abraham." The name is spoken twice to engage his attention; and perhaps the suddenness of the call made him draw back his hand just as he was going to strike his son. "And Abraham answered, Here am I" (verse 11).

B. The Message of the Angel of the Lord.

"And He said, Lay not thine hand upon the lad, neither do thou anything unto him: for now I know that thou fearest God, seeing thou hast not withheld thy son, thine only son from Me" (verse 12). Here it was that Abraham received his son Isaac from the dead in a figure. He was in effect offered upon the altar and God looked upon him as offered and given unto Him. Now it was that Abraham's faith, being tried, was found more precious than gold purified seven times in the fire.

C. The Confirmation of God's Promise.

Now as a reward of grace, though not of debt, for this signal act of obedience, by an oath, God gives and confirms the promise that in his seed all the nations of the earth should be blessed (verses 17-19). With what comfort may we suppose Abraham and Isaac went down from the mount and returned to the young men! With what joy may we imagine he went home and related to Sarah all the things which had taken place.

CONCLUSION

We are all fallen creatures and do not love God or Christ as we ought to do. If you admire Abraham's offering up his son, how much more ought you to extol, magnify, and adore the love of God, who so loved the world as to give His only begotten Son, Christ Jesus our Lord, "that whosoever believeth in Him should not perish, but have everlasting life" (John 3:16)? May we not well cry out, Now we know, O Lord, that Thou hast loved us, since Thou hast not withheld Thine only Son from us.

4

The Beloved of God

*And of Benjamin, he said, The beloved of
the Lord shall dwell in safety by Him; and
the Lord shall cover him all day long, and
he shall dwell between His shoulders.*
— Deuteronomy 33:12

If you read this chapter you will find how various,
yet special, are the blessings which, in a prophetic strain, Moses
foretells should attend particular persons or tribes. I have been
reading them over, and although I admire them all, I was at a loss
from which to speak, until the blessing of Benjamin fixed my
attention, not only as sweet, but also instructing.

I. THE IDENTIFICATION OF THE BELOVED OF GOD.

A. An Erroneous Notion.

Some say that the beloved of the Lord signifies all the men
that were ever born into the world. That is a broad bridge to
take them in, but broad bridges are not always the strongest
bridges in the world. Some assert that Judas was as much beloved as Peter or any other of the apostles.

B. The Biblical View.

The beloved of the Lord are the men that the Scriptures always speak of whose constant uniform character is they love
God. It is spoken of all the people of God. God help us to
apply it to ourselves. The love which God has for the world
is quite different from His love for His own children.

II. THE EVIDENCES OF BEING BELOVED OF GOD.

A. Abhorrence and Renunciation of Self-righteousness.

We are the beloved of the Lord if we are brought to abhor and renounce that which stands between us and the Lord; I mean our cursed self-righteousness. Can I prove that I have renounced my own plans, that I am sick of them, as well as my sins? None but the beloved of the Lord see this; an enemy may have this in his head, but only a friend of the Lord has it in his heart.

B. Love for the Children of God.

If I am beloved of the Lord, having His love in my heart, I will show it by loving those He has loved. As soon as we hear of a sinner turning to God it will rejoice us, and we shall be like the angels in heaven who rejoice over one sinner's repentance more than over ninety-nine just persons who need no repentance (Luke 15:7).

C. Hated by the World.

"If ye were of the world, the world would love his own: but because ye are not of the world, but I have chosen you out of the world, therefore the world hateth you" (John 15:19). You love the Lord and not be hated as was your Lord! I do not say that all are hated alike. In proportion to our successes will we be hated.

D. Living Victoriously over the World.

If I am beloved of the Lord, I really shall live above the world. I remember a dear friend once sent me word how busy he was morning and night, up early and late. "Perhaps," he said, "you will think by this account I am worldly"; but he continued, "No sir, I thank God that my heart is above the world." God grant we may thus prove we love God!

E. Fear of Offending God.

They that love the Lord will endeavor to keep from offending God, not for fear of being condemned, but because sin caused the death of God's Son. There are a great many people who abstain from sin for fear of punishment; but hear what Joseph said, "How can I do this great wickedness and sin against God" (Genesis 39:9), the God who loves me.

F. Willing Service for the Lord.

If we are the beloved of the Lord we shall be willing to work for the Lord. I knew a lady who wanted to be further employed in the service of God. Said she, If Christ would but help me to do such and such a thing I have in view, I would dedicate myself more and more to His honor. A true Christian loves thus to be employed.

G. Desire to See Jesus.

If we have the love of God in our hearts the bent of our minds will be, When shall I see "Him whom my soul loves"? "I am in a strait betwixt two," says Paul; the word signifies a strong intense desire "to be with Christ, which is far better" (Philippians 1:23).

III. A TEMPTATION OF THE BELOVED OF GOD.

A. The Nature of the Temptation.

Can I think God loves me when I am poor or afflicted? If I am beloved of the Lord, how is it that my friends are against me; that my children instead of being a blessing are breaking my heart? If I am beloved of the Lord why have I so many domestic trials; why am I harassed with blasphemous thoughts?

B. The Reminder Concerning the Temptation.

"Whom the Lord loveth He chasteneth, and scourgeth every son whom He receiveth" (Hebrews 12:6). Jesus was never more beloved of His Father than when He cried, "My God! My God! why hast Thou forsaken Me?" (Matthew 27:46) or in the Garden sweating great drops of blood as He cried, "Father, if it be possible, let this cup pass from Me" (Matthew 26:39; Luke 22:44).

IV. THE BLESSINGS OF THE BELOVED OF GOD.

A. They Shall Dwell Safely upon the Earth.

What is to be done to those that are beloved of the Lord? Here it is, "they shall dwell in safety." Why? "They shall dwell between His shoulders." Will God indeed dwell upon the earth? Yes, He dwells in my earthly heart made heavenly by the grace of God. Says the Lord, "I am thy shield" (Genesis 15:1).

B. They Shall Dwell Eternally in Heaven.

Those who are lovers of the Lord Jesus shall dwell safely with God on earth and eternally with Him in heaven. God loves and smiles upon His children and therefore they shall dwell in safety.

CONCLUSION

If any of you who have not the marks of being beloved of the Lord are awakened and convinced, the Lord grant you may not rest until you are God's beloved. Come, throw yourself upon Christ and say, "Lord, pardon my iniquities, for they are great."

5

Family Religion

> *As for me and my home, we will serve
> the Lord.* — Joshua 24:15

THESE WORDS contain the holy resolution of Joshua,
who in a most moving, affectionate discourse recounted to the
Israelites the great things God had done for them, and now comes
to draw a proper inference from what he had been delivering and
acquaint them, in the most pressing terms, that since God had
been so gracious to them, they could do no less than dedicate
themselves and families to God.

I. THE RESPONSIBILITY OF THE HEAD OF THE FAMILY IN RELATION TO FAMILY RELIGION.

A. The Character of His Responsibility.

Every head of a family ought to look upon himself as obliged to
act in three capacities: as a prophet to instruct; as a priest to
pray for and with; as a king to govern, direct and provide
for them.

B. The Importance of His Responsibility.

However indifferent some heads of families may be about it,
they may be assured that God will require a due discharge of
these offices at their hands. For if, as the apostle argues, he
that does not provide for his own in temporal things, "hath
denied the faith, and is worse than an infidel" (I Timothy
5:8); to what greater degree of apostasy must he have ar-
rived who takes no thought to provide for the spiritual welfare
of his family.

C. Examples of Meeting the Responsibility.

What precedents men who neglect their duty in this particular can plead for such omission I cannot tell. Doubtless not the example of holy Job (Job 1:5). Nor can they plead the practice of good old Joshua who in the text we find as much concerned for his household's welfare as his own. Nor that of Cornelius who feared God not only himself but with all his house (Acts 10:2). If Christians had the spirit of Job, Joshua, and the Gentile centurion, they would act like them.

II. THE NATURE OF FAMILY RELIGION.

A. Reading God's Word to the Family.

"Search the Scriptures, for in them ye think ye have eternal life" (John 5:39) is a precept given by our blessed Lord to all; but much more so ought every head of a family to think it in a peculiar manner spoken to himself, because he ought to look upon himself as a prophet and therefore bound to instruct those under his charge in the knowledge of the Word of God. This was the order God gave to Israel (Deuteronomy 6:6-7).

B. Family Prayers.

This is a duty, although as much neglected, yet as absolutely necessary as reading the Scriptures. Reading the Bible is a good preparative for prayer, as prayer is an excellent means to render reading effectual. The reason why every head of a family should join both of these exercises together is plain, because a head of a family cannot perform his priestly office without performing the duty of family prayer.

C. Family Instruction.

Every head of a family should catechize and instruct the entire household and bring them up in the nurture and admonition of the Lord. This is seen in God's commendation of Abraham: "I know that he will command his children and household after him, to keep the way of the Lord, to do justice and judgment" (Genesis 18:19). Parents are commanded in the New Testament to "bring up their children in the nurture and admonition of the Lord" (Ephesians 6:4).

III. THE MOTIVES FOR FAMILY RELIGION.

A. Gratitude to God.

The first motive I shall mention is the duty of gratitude which you who are heads of families owe to God. Providence has given to you a goodly heritage, above many of your fellow-men. Therefore, out of a principle of gratitude you ought to endeavor, as much as in you lies, to make every person of your respective households to call upon Him as long as they live. Thus did Abraham and Joshua. Let us go and do likewise.

B. Love for the Family.

If gratitude to God will not, I think love and pity for your children should move you with your families to serve the Lord. Most people express a great fondness for their children and provide, therefore, for their bodily needs; but they forget the salvation of their immortal souls. Is this their way of expressing their fondness for their children? Then was Delilah fond of Samson when she delivered him into the hands of the Philistines.

C. Self Interest.

This weighs greatly with you in other matters; then be persuaded to let it have a due and full influence on you in this. If it has, and you have faith as a grain of mustard seed, how can you avoid believing that promoting family religion will be the best means to promote your own temporal as well as eternal welfare? "Godliness has the promise of the life that now is, as well as that which is to come" (I Timothy 4:8).

D. Terrors of the Lord.

Let a consideration of the terrors of the Lord persuade you to put into practice the pious resolution of the text. Remember, the time will come, and that perhaps very shortly, when we must all appear before the judgment-seat of Christ where we must give a solemn and strict account how we have conducted ourselves in our respective families in this world. How will you endure to see your children, who ought to be your joy and crown of rejoicing in the day of our Lord Jesus Christ, coming out as so many witnesses against you?

CONCLUSION

I hope you have been in some measure convinced by what has been said of the importance of family religion and therefore are ready to cry out: "God forbid that we should forsake the Lord; we will (with our households) serve the Lord" (Joshua 24:16, 21). That there may always be such a heart in you, let me exhort all heads of families often to reflect on the worth of their own souls and the infinite ransom, Christ's blood, which has been paid for them.

6

Soul Dejection

Why art thou cast down, O my soul, and why art thou disquieted within me? Hope thou in God, for I shall yet praise Him, for the help of His countenance.
— **Psalm 42:5**

I HONOR DAVID when I see him yonder tending a few sheep. I admire the young stripling when I see him come out with his sling and stones and aiming at the head of Goliath, the enemy of God; or when exalted and filling the seat of justice. However, to me he never appears greater than when he is bowed down in low circumstances, beset on every side, struggling between sense and faith; and like the sun after an eclipse, breaking forth with greater luster to all the spectators.

I. ASPECTS OF SOUL DEJECTION.

A. The Psalmist Asks the Cause of His Soul Dejection.

Suppose you understand the words as a question. "Why art thou cast down, O my soul" though thou art in such circumstances? What is the cause of being so dejected? The word implies that he was sinking under the weight of his present burden, like a person stooping under a load that lies on his shoulders; and the consequence of this pressure without was turmoil, uneasiness, and anxiety within. There is a connection between soul and body that when one is disordered the other sympathizes with it.

B. The Psalmist Chides Himself for His Soul Dejection.

You may understand it as chiding himself: How foolish is it to be thus drooping and dejected; how improper for one

31

favored of God with so many providences and special privileges to stoop and be made subject to every temptation. Why do you give your enemies cause to find fault with Christianity on account of your gloomy looks and the disquietude of your heart? You see he speaks not to others, but to himself. I would to God we did thus learn to begin with ourselves.

II. THE CAUSES FOR SOUL DEJECTION.

A. Conviction of Sin.

Some poor soul will say, I am cast down with a sense of sin, the guilt of it, the enmity of it; the very aggravated circumstances that attend it appear and set themselves in battle-array before me. Once I thought I had no sin, or that sin was not so exceeding sinful; but I now find it such a burden, I could almost say with Cain, "it is greater than I can bear." Perhaps you could say as one man said when under conviction of sin, "I believe God cannot be just unless He damn my wicked soul."

B. Unfaithfulness to God.

I hear someone say, I am cast down because after I knew God to be my God, after I knew Jesus to be my king, the devil and my unbelieving heart threw me down again. Would not God have me cast down? Would He not have me disquieted? You are gone far from your Father's house. If nothing else will do, may your Father whip you back home! Tender hearts, when they reflect how it was once, are cast down.

C. Temptation.

You may say, I am cast down because I am wearied with temptation. I am haunted with this and that evil suggestion until I am a terror to myself. Is it unbelief that dogs you wherever you go? Although it be night, there is some moon, blessed be God, or some stars. If there is a fog that you cannot see, God can quiet His people in the dark; He will make the enemy flee. God will comfort you and punish the devil for tempting you.

D. Trials.

You may say, I have one affliction after another; no sooner is one trial gone, but another follows. I think I shall have a little rest, the tormentor will not come near today, but no sooner has this been said, but another storm comes and the clouds return after the rain. With such experiences we think we must be cast down and ought to be disquieted. This was David's case, "All Thy waves and Thy billows are gone over me" (verse 7). I believe after that there were more waves to come than he had yet felt.

E. Fear.

Perhaps some of you may be cast down with fear, not of death only, but of judgment. I believe many people die a thousand times for fear of dying once. Poor soul, leave this to God. He will take care of your dying hour. "Having loved His own, He loves them to the end." He is a faithful, unchangeable friend that sticketh closer than a brother.

III. TRIUMPH OVER SOUL DEJECTION.

A. The Dejected Psalmist Goes to God.

He goes to God with his case, "O my God, my soul is cast down within me" (verse 6). Oh, that we would learn when in these moods to go more to God and less to man; then we should find more relief and Christianity would be less dishonored.

B. The Dejected Psalmist Trusts in God.

See how faith triumphs in the midst of all. No sooner does unbelief raise its head but faith immediately knocks it down. A never-failing maxim is here proposed, "Hope thou in God," trust in God, believe in Him. I am sure, and all of you who know Jesus Christ are persuaded of it too, that all our troubles arise from our unbelief. Unbelief is an injurious bar to comfort and a source of tormenting fear. On the contrary, faith bears everything.

C. The Dejected Psalmist Assures Himself in God.

The devil tells me my trouble is so great I shall never lift
up my head again; but unbelief and Satan are liars. "I shall
yet praise Him." My God will carry me through all. I shall
praise Him for casting me down; I shall praise Him for that
which is the cause of all my unrest. I shall see Him again and
be favored with those transforming views with which He favored me in times past.

CONCLUSION

Oh that I could persuade one poor soul to fly to Jesus Christ!
Make Him your refuge and then, however you may be cast down,
you "shall yet praise Him." God help those who have believed to
hope more and more in His salvation until faith be turned into
vision and hope into fruition. Even so, Lord Jesus.

7

Christk the Believer's Husband

For thy Maker is thy husband.
— Isaiah 54:5

T HE WORDS of our text point out to us a relationship
which not only comprehends, but, in respect to nearness and dear-
ness, exceeds all other relationships. I mean that of a husband. Although the words were originally spoken to the Jews, yet they are
undoubtedly applicable to all believers in all ages. When enlarged
upon in a proper manner they will afford us suitable matter of
discourse for sinners and saints and for those who once walked in
the light of His countenance but are now backslidden from Him.

I. THE REQUIREMENTS FOR THIS RELATIONSHIP.

A. Freedom from all Pre-engagements.

We are all by nature born under and wedded to the Law as
a covenant of works. Hence it is that we are so fond of, and
artfully go about to establish a righteousness of our own. But
before we can say, "our Maker is our husband," we must be
made free from our old husband the Law; we must renounce
our own righteousness, our own doings and performances, in
point of dependence, whether in whole or part, as dross for
the excellency of the knowledge of Christ.

B. Mutual Consent.

Before we can say that "our Maker is our husband" we must
be made willing people in the day of God's power. We must
be sweetly and effectually persuaded by the Holy Spirit of
God that the glorious Emmanuel is willing to accept us just

as we are and also that we are willing to accept Him upon His own terms, yea, upon any terms.

C. Union.

We are called Christians after Christ's name, because made partakers of Christ's nature. Out of His fulness believers receive grace for grace. Therefore the marriage state, especially by Paul, is frequently used as a figure of the real and vital union between Christ and believers. This is termed in Ephesians 5:32, "a great mystery." Great as it is, we must all experience it before we can say, "Our Maker is our husband."

II. THE DUTIES IN CONNECTION WITH THIS RELATIONSHIP.

A. Reverence.

"Let the wife see that she reverence her husband" (Ephesians 5:33). May I not apply this caution to you who are married to Jesus Christ? See to it that you reverence and respect your husband. I say, *see to it*. For the devil will be often suggesting to you hard and mean thoughts about your husband (Christ). Besides, in the eyes of the world, Jesus Christ has no form or comeliness. Therefore, unless you watch and pray you will not keep up such high thoughts of Him as He deserves.

B. Worthy Walk.

"The woman is the glory of the man" (I Corinthians 11:7) even as the church is the glory of Christ. Agreeable to this are the Apostle's words, "Whether you eat or drink, or whatsoever you do, do all the glory of God" (I Corinthians 10:31) and "walk worthy of God" (I Thessalonians 2:12). You are His glory and you should so walk that He will be glorified in you.

C. Subjection.

Since wives are to be subject to their own husbands, how much more ought believers, whether men or women, to be subject to Jesus Christ. He is the head of the church and has purchased her by His blood. Believers therefore are not their own, but are under the highest obligations to glorify and obey Christ in their bodies and souls which are His.

D. Faithfulness.

How carefully ought Christians to keep their souls chaste, pure, and undefiled. There is such a thing as spiritual adultery (James 4:4). Hence it is that the apostle John, in the most endearing manner, exhorts believers to "keep themselves from idols" (I John 5:31). Every time we place our affections upon anything more than Christ we commit spiritual adultery. For then we allow a creature to rival the Creator.

E. Fruitfulness.

If we are married to Jesus Christ we must be fruitful in every good work. We are dead to the law and married to Christ in order "that we should bring forth fruit unto God" (Romans 7:4). Titus is commanded to exhort believers to "be careful to maintain good works" (3:8). "Herein," says Christ, "is My Father glorified, that ye bear much fruit" (John 15:8).

III. THE CONDITION OF THE PERSONS WHO HAVE NEVER EXPERIENCED THIS RELATIONSHIP.

A. They Are Married to the Law.

If you are not married to Jesus Christ you are married to the Law. Do you not hear, you that seek to be justified in the sight of God by your works, what God says to those who are under the Law? "Cursed is every one that continueth not in all things that are written in the book of the Law, to do them" (Galatians 3:10).

B. They Are Married to the World.

Why are you so wedded to the world? Did it ever prove faithful or satisfactory to any of its votaries? The sum total of worldly happiness is stated by Solomon: "All is vanity and vexation of spirit" (Ecclesiastes 1:14). A greater than Solomon has informed us that a man's life does not consist in the things he possesses (Luke 12:15).

C. They Are Married to the Flesh.

What reasons can you give for being wedded to your lusts?
Might not the ancient galley slaves as reasonably be wedded
to their chains?   Do not your lusts fetter your souls?   Do
they not have dominion over you?   Do they not say, Come, and
ye come; Go, and ye go; Do this, and ye do it?   Is not he or
she who lives in pleasure dead while he lives?

D. They Are Married to the Devil.

How can you bear the thoughts of being wedded to the devil,
as is every natural man?   How can you bear to be ruled by
one who is such a professed, open enemy to the most high and
holy God?   He will make a drudge of you while you live and
be your companion in endless and extreme torment after death.

CONCLUSION

The Lord Jesus is the fountain of wisdom and makes all who
come to Him wise unto salvation.   As He is wise, so is He holy.
Therefore He is called the Holy One of Israel.   Nor is His beauty
inferior to His wisdom and holiness. "He is altogether lovely." He
is altogether loving.   His name and His nature is love.   He manifested His love by dying for us.

8

The Potter and the Clay

> *The word which came to Jeremiah from the Lord, saying, Arise, and go down to the potter's house, and there I will cause thee to hear my words. Then I went down to the potter's house, and, behold, he wrought a work on the wheels. And the vessel that he made of clay was marred in the hand of the potter: so he made it again another vessel, as seemed good to the potter to make it. Then the word of the Lord came to me, saying, O house of Israel, cannot I do with you as this potter? saith the Lord. Behold, as the clay is in the potter's hand, so are ye in mine hand, O house of Israel.* — Jeremiah 18:1-6

SOMETIMES God was pleased to send a prophet on some special errand and while he was thus employed a particular message was given to him which he was ordered to deliver to all the inhabitants of the land. An instructive instance of this kind is recorded in the passage we are now to consider. But what Jehovah here says of Israel in general is applicable to every man individually.

I. UNREGENERATE MAN IS A PIECE OF MARRED CLAY.

A. Man's Original State.

1. *The Scriptural statement.* "And God said, Let us make man in our image, after our likeness. So God created man in

His own image, in the image of God created He him" (Genesis 1:26, 27).

2. *The Scriptural statement explained.* Man was originally made upright. He was created "after God" in knowledge, as well as righteousness and true holiness.

B. Man's Present State.

Man soon fell from his primeval dignity and by that fall the divine image became defaced.

1. *His knowledge is affected.* In respect to natural things man's understanding is evidently darkened. He can know only a little and that knowledge which he can acquire is with much weariness of the flesh. In respect to spiritual things his understanding is not only darkened, but has become darkness itself.

2. *His will is perverted.* Man is the image of God; undoubtedly before the fall man had no other will but his Maker's. There was not the least disunion between them. Now man has a will as directly contrary to the will of God as light is contrary to darkness, or heaven to hell.

3. *His affections are defiled.* Man's affections when first placed in Eden were always kept within proper bounds and fixed upon proper objects. Now the scene is changed. We are now naturally full of vile affections. We love what we should hate and hate what we should love; we fear what we should hope for and hope for what we should fear.

4. *His conscience is corrupted.* In the soul of the first man Adam conscience was, undoubtedly, the candle of the Lord and enabled him rightly and instantaneously to discern between right and wrong. Some remains of this are yet left, but it burns dimly and is easily covered or extinguished.

5. *His reason is depraved.* There will come a time when those who despise and oppose divine revelation will find that what they now call reason is only reason depraved and incapable of itself to guide us into the way of peace or

show the way of salvation, as the men of Sodom were unable to find Lot's door when they were struck with blindness.

6. *His body is in a state of humiliation.* Without attempting to be wise above what is written, we may venture to affirm that originally man had a body which knew no sin, sickness, nor pain; but now its primitive strength and glory has departed.

II. THE NECESSITY FOR THE UNREGENERATE MAN'S RENEWAL.

A. The Fact of Man's Present Condition.

I have been purposely explicit on the unregenerate man's present condition so we may venture to say, Grant the foregoing doctrine to be true, then you cannot deny the necessity of man's renewal.

B. The Hope of Heaven.

1. *Two concepts of heaven.*
   a. Because the Scriptures, in condescension to the weakness of our capacities, describe heaven by images taken from earthly delights and human grandeur, therefore men are apt to carry their thoughts no higher.

   b. Heaven is a state as well as a place. Consequently, unless you are previously disposed by a suitable state of mind you cannot be happy in heaven.

2. *The necessity of a moral change.* To make us ready to be blissful partakers of the heavenly company this "marred clay," our depraved natures, must undergo a universal moral change. Old things must pass away, all things must become new.

III. THE METHOD OF THE UNREGENERATE MAN'S RENEWAL.

A. Negatively Stated.

1. *It is more than moral persuasion.* If it is asked how this great change is to be effected, I answer, not by the mere

dint and force of moral persuasion. This is good in its place, but it will not produce the necessary change.

2. *It is more than the power of free will.* "No man," says Christ, "can come to Me unless the Father draw him" (John 6:44). Our own free will, if exercised, may restrain us from committing evil and place us in the way of conversion; but after exerting our efforts, and we are bound in duty to do so, we will find it true that "man since the fall has no power to turn to God."

B. Positively Stated.

1. *It is the work of the Holy Spirit.* The heavenly Potter is the Spirit of God, the third person of the adorable Trinity. This is the Spirit who moved on the face of the waters, who overshadowed the holy virgin. He must move upon the chaos of our souls in order to be sons of God.

2. *It is a miraculous work of the Holy Spirit.* This miracle of miracles, turning the soul to God, will continue until time shall be no more. True believers are said to be born from above, to be born not of blood, nor of the will of man, but of God (John 3:3, 7; 1:13).

CONCLUSION

To produce this new creation, Jesus left His Father's bosom, led a persecuted life, died an ignominious and accursed death, rose again, and is seated on His Father's right hand. All His precepts and providences, all divine revelation center in these two points: our fallen condition; and to begin, carry on, and complete a change in our souls.

9

The Lord Our Righteousness

The Lord our righteousness.
— Jeremiah 23:6

THE RIGHTEOUSNESS of Jesus Christ seems to be one of the first lessons that God taught man after the fall. The coats that God made to put on our first parents were types of the application of the merits of the righteousness of our Lord to the believers' hearts. We may infer that those coats came from animals slain in sacrifice in commemoration of the great sacrifice upon Calvary.

I. THE IDENTIFICATION OF THE LORD.

A. He is Jesus Christ.

The person mentioned in the text under the character of Lord is Jesus Christ. *The Lord our righteousness* is the *righteous branch* of verse 5 and all agree that the righteous branch is Jesus Christ.

B. He is God.

Since the word LORD properly belongs to Christ, He must be God. For as you have it in the margins of your Bibles, the word LORD is in the original *Jehovah* which is the essential title of God Himself. Therefore, He must be very God of very God, or as the Apostle devoutly expresses it, "God blessed forever" (Romans 9:5).

II. THE EXPLANATIONS OF THE LORD OUR RIGHTEOUSNESS.

A. Man's Need.

The third chapter of Genesis gives us a full but mournful account how our first parents sinned and thereby stood in need

43

of a better righteousness than their own in order to procure their future acceptance with God.

B. God's Provision.

Christ not only died, but lived; not only suffered, but obeyed for or in the stead of sinners. Both of these jointly make up that complete righteousness which is to be imputed to us, as the disobedience of our first parents was made ours by imputation. In this sense,, and no other, are we to understand that parallel which Saint Paul draws in the fifth chapter of Romans between the first and second Adam.

III. THE CONSIDERATION OF THE OBJECTIONS AGAINST THE DOCTRINE OF THE LORD OUR RIGHTEOUSNESS.

A. "The doctrine of imputed righteousness is destructive of good works."

Never was there a reformation brought about in the church, but by preaching of the doctrine of Christ's imputed righteousness. It excludes works from being any cause of our justification in the sight of God. It requires good works as a proof of our having this righteousness imputed to us and as a declarative evidence of our justification in the sight of men. Then how can the doctrine of imputed righteousness be a doctrine leading to licentiousness?

B. "The doctrine of imputed righteousness is not the teaching of the Sermon on the Mount."

In this sermon our Lord speaks of inward piety, such as purity of heart, and hungering and thirsting after righteousness, and then recommends good works as an evidence of our having His righteousness imputed to us, and these graces and divine tempers wrought in our hearts. Then He adds, Think not that I am come to destroy the moral law — I come not to destroy, to take away the force of it as a rule of life, but to fulfill, to obey it.

C. "The doctrine of imputed righteousness is not the teaching of Mark 10:17-22."

Our Lord by referring the young man to the commandments
did not in the least hint that his morality would recommend
him to God's mercy and favor. He intended thereby to make
the Law his schoolmaster to bring him to Himself; that the
young man, seeing how he had broken every commandment,
might thereby be convinced of his own insufficiency and the
absolute necessity of looking for a better righteousness whereon he might depend for eternal life.

D. "The doctrine of imputed righteousness is not the teaching of Matthew 25:34-36."

This refers to rewards and not salvation. That the people did
not depend on these good actions for their justification in the
sight of God is evident from verses 37-39. They were so far
from depending on their works for justification in the sight of
God that they were filled as it were with a holy blushing to
think that our Lord should mention and reward them for their
poor works of faith and labors of love.

IV. THE EVIL CONSEQUENCES OF THE REJECTION OF THE DOCTRINE OF THE LORD OUR RIGHTEOUSNESS.

A. The Rejectors Turn the Word of God into a Lie.

It would be endless to enumerate the number of Scripture
texts that must be false if this doctrine is not true. Let it
suffice to affirm in general that if we deny an imputed righteousness we may as well deny a divine revelation all at once.
For it is the *alpha* and *omega,* the beginning and the end of the
book of God. We must either disbelieve the Bible or believe
what the prophet has spoken in the text, "the Lord our righteousness."

B. The Rejector Becomes a Setter-forth of Unscriptural
Teaching.

Suppose I told you that you must intercede with saints in order
that they may intercede with God for you; or, that the death

of Christ was not sufficient without our death added to it? Might you not then justly call me a setter-forth of strange doctrines? Is it not equally absurd and blasphemous to join our obedience, either wholly or in part, with the obedience of Christ — both active and passive?

C. The Rejector Is Doomed to Eternal Torment.

If there be no such thing as the doctrine of an imputed righteousness then those who hold it and bring forth fruit unto holiness are safe. If there be such a thing (as there certainly is), what will become of you who deny it? It is no difficult matter to determine. Your portion must be in the lake of fire and brimstone forever and ever; since you will rely upon your works, by your works you shall be judged.

CONCLUSION

Can anything appear more reasonable, even according to your own way of arguing, than the doctrine of "the Lord our righteousness"? Have you not felt a convincing power go along with the Word? Why then will you not believe on the Lord Jesus Christ in order that He may become the Lord your righteousness? For think you, O sinners, that you will be able to stand in the day of judgment if Christ is not your righteousness? No, that alone is the wedding garment in which you must appear.

10

Christ's Everlasting Righteousness

And to bring in everlasting righteousness
— Daniel 9:24

T HE WORDS chosen for the text of the present meditation
contain part of a revelation made to the prophet Daniel. If you
look back to the beginning of this chapter (verses 2-4), you will
find how this good man was employed when God was pleased to
give him this revelation. He made the Bible his constant study;
for it is the Bible we are to understand by what is here termed
books. He prayed and confessed his sins and those of the people.

I. THE EXPLANATION OF RIGHTEOUSNESS.

A. There Is a Righteousness which Signifies Moral Honesty.

In various passages of Scripture the word righteousness has no
other meaning or, at least, bears the meaning of moral honesty,
that is, doing justice between man and man. When Paul
reasoned with Felix about righteousness (Acts 24:25), he
preached to him of the necessity of doing justice because he
had been an unjust man; and he put before him the judgment
to come in order to make him come to Christ for deliverance
from the bad consequences of that judgment.

B. There Is a Righteousness which Signifies Holiness.

It likewise signifies inward holiness which is wrought in us
by the blessed Spirit of God.

C. There Is a Righteousness which Is Imputed.

I believe the word righteousness in the text signifies an
imputed righteousness, or the righteousness of the Lord Jesus

Christ which is imputed to poor sinners when they believe in
Christ as Lord and Savior. By *righteousness* I understand all
that Christ has done and all that Christ has suffered: put these
two together and they make up the righteousness of the Lord
Jesus Christ. Blessed be God for this righteousness! Blessed
be God for the adjective which in the text is used with this
righteousness — everlasting righteousness.

II. THE REASON CHRIST'S RIGHTEOUSNESS IS CALLED EVERLASTING.

A. Because It Extends to Mankind from Eternity.

This should deepen our love to God, to think that from all the
ages of eternity God had thoughts of us; God intended the
Lord Jesus Christ to save our souls; hence it is that God, to
endear Jeremiah to Him, tells him, "I have loved thee with an
everlasting love." All that we receive in time flows from that
inexhaustible fountain, God's everlasting love. Therefore, the
righteousness of Jesus Christ may properly be called an everlasting righteousness, because God intended it from everlasting.

B. Because All Saints Are Saved by Christ's Righteousness.

It is called an everlasting righteousness because the efficacy of
Christ's death took place immediately upon Adam's fall. The
righteousness of Jesus Christ may be called an everlasting
righteousness because all of the saints that have been saved or
ever will be saved are all saved by the righteousness of Christ.
It was through the faith in Christ that Abel was saved; it was
through the sacrifice of Christ that Abraham and the prophets
were accepted. Since persons under the law and under the
gospel are saved through Christ, therefore, Christ's righteousness may be called an everlasting righteousness.

C. Because Its Efficacy Will Continue to the End of Time.

The righteousness of Jesus Christ is called an everlasting
righteousness because the efficacy thereof will continue until
time shall be no more. The efficacy of the Lord Jesus' blood,
death, and atonement is as great and effectual now to the salvation of poor sinners as when He bowed His head and gave

up His spirit. Whosoever believes on Him now shall see His power, shall taste of His grace, and shall be actually saved by Him the same as if he had been in company with those who saw Him expiring.

D. Because Its Benefit Endures to Everlasting Life.

Christ's righteousness may be called an everlasting righteousness because the benefit of it is to endure to everlasting life. No wicked demon nor your own depraved heart shall be able to separate you from the love of God. God has loved you, He has fixed His heart upon you, and having loved His own, He loves them unto the end. Those who once take hold of Christ's righteousness shall be saved everlastingly by Him. Our salvation depends not upon our own free will, but upon God's free grace.

III. THE SIGNIFICANCE OF THE WORDS "TO BRING IN."

A. It Is Our Lord's Promulgation and Proclamation of His Righteousness to the World.

His righteousness was brought in under the law; but then it was brought in under types and shadows. But Jesus Christ brought life and immortality to light by the gospel. The light of Moses was only twilight; the light of the gospel is like the sun at noonday. Therefore, Christ may be said to bring in this everlasting righteousness, because He proclaimed it to the world and commanded it to be preached that God sent His Son into the world that the world through Him might be saved.

B. It Is Our Lord's Working Out His Righteousness on the Cross.

Again, the Lord Jesus Christ brought in this righteousness as He wrought it out for sinners upon the cross. Although man is justified, in God's mind, from all eternity, yet it was not actually brought in until the Lord Jesus Christ pronounced the words, "It is finished"; the grand consummation! Then Jesus brought it in. A new and living way was opened into the holy of holies for poor sinners, by the blood of Christ.

C. It Is the Holy Spirit's Bringing Christ's Righteousness into a Man's Soul.

All that Christ has done, all that Christ has suffered will do us no good unless by the Spirit of God it is brought into our souls. As one expresses it, "an unapplied Christ is no Christ at all." To hear of a Christ dying for sinners will only increase one's damnation, will only sink him deeper into hell, unless he has ground to say by a work of grace wrought in his heart that the Lord Jesus has brought this home to him.

CONCLUSION

Are any of you depending on a righteousness of your own? Do any of you think to save yourselves by your own doings? I say to you, your righteousness shall perish with you. The righteousness of Jesus Christ is an everlasting righteousness wrought out for the very chief of sinners. Christ's righteousness will cover, His blood will cleanse you from the guilt of all sin. Oh, come, come! How will you stand before an angry God without the righteousness of the Lord Jesus Christ?

11

The Temptation of Christ

> *Then was Jesus led up of the Spirit into the wilderness, to be tempted of the devil.*
> — Matthew 4:1

LET US with serious attention consider when, where and how our Savior fought and overcame the devil. Matthew (4:1-11) is very particular in relating the preparations for, the beginning, the process, and issue of this important combat.

I. THE CIRCUMSTANCES OF THE TEMPTATION.

A. The Time.

1. *It was immediately following Christ's baptism.* In the close of chapter 3 we are told that Jesus was baptized and inaugurated to His mediatorial office by the opened heavens, descent of the Spirit and the voice from heaven.

2. *It was about the time of the beginning of Christ's public ministry.* He was about to show Himself openly unto Israel.

3. *It was when Christ was full of the Holy Spirit.* When He was full of the Holy Spirit (Luke 4:1), even then He was led with a holy unconstrained violence as a champion into the field to engage an enemy whom He was sure to conquer.

B. The Place.

1. *It was a lonesome wilderness.* But whither is this conqueror led? He is led into a lonesome, wide, howling wilderness. He was probably led, according to Matthew Henry, into the great wilderness of Sinai.

2. *It was a wild beast infested wilderness.* It was not only a lonesome wilderness, but inhabited, also, by wild beasts (Mark 1:13). Hither was our Lord led to pray and fast and meet His adversary.

C. The Conditions.

1. *He fasted.* Neither does He content Himself with praying, but He fasts also, and that forty days and forty nights (Matthew 4:2), even as Moses and Elijah had done many years before; it may be in the very same place.

2. *He hungered.* We may suppose that during these forty days our Lord felt no hunger. Converse with heaven to Him was instead of meat and drink; but "afterwards He was an hungered"; exceedingly so, no doubt. Now the important fight begins.

II. THE CONFLICT OF THE TEMPTATION.

A. The Nature of the Temptation

1. *To gender doubt.* Probably transformed into the appearance of an angel of light, Satan tempts our Lord to nothing less than to doubt that He is the Son of God. "If Thou be the Son of God" (verse 3).

2. *To encourage presumption.* Since Satan cannot draw Him to distrust or despair, he will now try to prevail on Him to presume. He takes Jesus to the pinnacle of the Temple in Jerusalem and bids Him to cast Himself down to prove His deity (verses 5-6).

3. *To appeal to pride.* In the third temptation Satan takes Christ into a high mountain and shows Him the kingdoms of the world and their glory; promising them to Him upon the condition of worshipping the Adversary (verses 8-9).

B. The Manner of Meeting the Temptations.

1. *The use of God's Word.* Although the Lord Jesus had the Spirit of God without measure and might have made use of a thousand other ways, yet He answered the tempter with texts of Scripture. Each time He quoted from Deuteronomy.

2. *The use of the word of rebuke.* After the third temptation our Lord, filled with a holy resentment, said "Get thee hence, Satan" (verse 10). Get thee hence, I will bear thy insolence no longer.

C. The Outcome of the Temptation.

1. *Christ victorious.* Now the battle is over. The important combat is ended. Jesus has won the field.

2. *Satan defeated.* Satan is routed and totally put to flight. "Then," when the devil found that Jesus could withstand even the golden bait, the lust of the eye and the pride of life, in the last two, as well as the lust of the flesh in the first temptation, despairing of the least success, "he leaveth Him."

III. THE CONSIDERATION OF THE LESSONS OF THE TEMPTATION.

A. Solitude May be Harmful.

1. *Proper solitude is profitable.* Was our Lord violently beset in the wilderness? Then we may learn that however profitable solitude may be when used in due season, yet when carried too far is hurtful.

2. *Extreme solitude encourages temptation.* Woe be to him that is always alone! He has not another to lift him when he falls or to advise him when he is tempted. Lord, keep us from leading ourselves into this temptation and support and deliver us when led by Thy providence into it.

B. The Path of Preparation for Christian Service.

1. *Exemplified by our Lord.* Did our Lord by prayer, fasting, and temptation prepare himself for His public ministry? Surely then all those who profess to be inwardly moved by the Holy Spirit to take upon them the office and administration of the church should be prepared in the same manner.

2. *The reason for this need.* Without a knowledge of Satan's devices, a minister will be like a physician who prescribes to the sick without having studied medicine. If you would be useful in comforting broken hearts and wounded souls, prepare yourselves for manifold temptation.

C. The Time of Poverty Is the Time of Temptation.

1. *The nature of the temptation.* Let those of you who are reduced to a low estate learn that an hour of poverty is an hour of temptation, not only to murmuring and doubting our sonship and Divine favor, but also to help ourselves by unlawful means.

2. *The responsibility of the tempted.* Remember that poverty and temptation are not marks of being cast off by God. Learn of Him not to distrust, but rather to trust in your heavenly Father.

D. The Successful Weapon Against Temptation.

1. *The Word of God.* Let us learn of our Lord to fight the devil with the Sword of the Spirit, which is the Word of God. We may say of it, as David did of Goliath's sword, "None like this."

2. *The power of the Word of God.* Had God's children observed to use the Scriptures correctly, how much strange fire would have been extinguished; how many imaginary revelations would have been detected; how many triumphs of Satan would have been prevented!

CONCLUSION

He who conquered for us in the wilderness will make us also more than conquerors over all trials and temptations and over death and hell itself, through His almighty, everlasting, and never failing love.

12

Christic the Support of the Tempted

Lead us not into temptation.
— Matthew 6:13

THE GREAT and important duty of every Christian is to
guard against all appearance of evil; to watch against the first
risings in the heart of evil and to guard our actions that they may
not be sinful or even seem to be so. It is true that the devil is continually tempting us, and our own evil hearts are ready to join
with the tempter, to make us fall into sins, that thereby he might
obtain a victory over us and we become his slaves. The Lord
Jesus seeing how His disciples and others are liable to be overcome by temptation advises them to pray that they might not be
led into it.

I. THE TEMPTER.

A. His Identification.

The tempter is Satan, the prince of the power of the air, he
that now rules in the children of disobedience (Ephesians 2:2).
He is an enemy of God and goodness, he is a hater of all truth.
For no other reason did he slander God in paradise. For no
other reason did he say to Eve, "You shall not surely die"
(Genesis 3:4).

B. His Character.

The tempter is full of malice, envy, and revenge; for what else
could enduce him to molest innocent man in Eden? The person that tempts you is remarkable for his subtilty: for not
having power given him from above, he is obliged to wait for

opportunities to betray us and to catch us by guile. Therefore he made use of the serpent to tempt our first parent. To lie in wait to deceive is another part of his character. Although this character is given of the devil, if we were to examine our own hearts we would find many of the tempter's characteristics legible in us.

II. THE TEMPTER'S REASONS FOR TEMPTING.

A. Because He Is Envious.

Why he tempts you is the second thing I am to show you. It is out of envy to you and to the Lord Jesus Christ.

B. Because He Wishes to Keep Men from Christ.

If he can keep you from laying hold by faith on Christ, he knows he has you safe enough. The more temptations you are under, and according to their nature and greatness, the more you are disturbed in your minds; and the more unsettled your thoughts and affections are, the more apt you are to conclude that He would not receive you. This is the policy of the tempter, to make you have low and dishonorable thoughts of Christ. Therefore, by degrees he works upon your minds insomuch that you become careless and indifferent about Christ. Nothing will please him more than to see you ruined and lost forever.

III. THE TEMPTER'S METHODS.

A. Flattery.

He endeavors to make you think sin is not so great as it is; that there is no occasion of being over-strict and that you are righteous over-much; that you are ostentatious, and will do yourselves harm by it and that you will destroy yourselves. He shows you the bait, but he hides the hook. He shows you the pleasures, profits, and advantages that attend the abundance of his world's goods; but he does not show you the crosses, losses, and vexations that you may have while you are in the enjoyment of the blessings of this world.

B. Doubts and Discouragements.

He throws doubts and discouragements in your mind, whether the way you are in is the true way or not. He may suggest, What! do you expect to be saved by Christ? Also, he may suggest, Christ did not die for you; you have been too great a sinner; you have lived in sin so long and committed such sins against Christ which He will not forgive.

C. Persecution.

When he finds he cannot allure in some way, he will try you by frowns and the terrors of this world. He will stir up people to point at you. He will stir them up to jeer, scoff, backbite, and hate you. Sometimes when the people of God are met to worship Him, Satan sends his agents, the scoffers, to disturb them.

IV. THE SECRET OF VICTORY OVER TEMPTATION.

A. Confession.

I shall now show you how earnest you ought to be with Jesus Christ, either not to suffer you to be led into temptation or to preserve you under it. Let me beseech you to go to Christ and tell Him how you are assaulted by the Evil One, who lies in wait for your souls. Tell Him you are not able to master the tempter in your own strength.

B. Prayer.

Beg the Lord Jesus' assistance and you will find Him ready to help you. He will give you strength to resist the fiery darts of the devil and therefore, you can nowhere find one so able to relieve you. He knows what it is to be tempted and He will give you the assistance of His Spirit to resist Satan, who will then flee from you. In Christ Jesus you have the strength you need. Fear not, for in the name of the Lord we shall overcome all our spiritual Amalekites. Let them rage, Jesus Christ has them in His power and they shall go no farther than He permits them.

C. Committal.

If Satan and his followers could do us all the mischief they desired, very few of us should be permitted to see our habitations any more; but blessed be God, we can commit ourselves to His protection. He has been our protector hitherto and He will be so still. Let us keep looking up unto Jesus.

CONCLUSION

You have found Jesus Christ assisting you and supporting you under all the temptations of this life, is not He the chiefest of ten thousand and the altogether lovely One? Now you see a form and beauty in Christ which you never saw before. Oh! how do you and I wish we had known Jesus sooner and that we had more of His love — it is condescending love; it is amazing love, it is forgiving love, it is dying love, it is exalted and interceding love, it is glorified love.

13

What Do You Think of Jesus Christ?

What think ye of Christ?
— **Matthew 22:42**

W HEN it pleased the eternal Son of God to tabernacle among men and preach the glad tidings of salvation to a fallen world, different opinions were entertained by different persons concerning Him as to His person and work. Thus today, professing Christians are sadly divided in their thoughts about Him. Therefore, to inform your consciences I will ask you a few questions concerning Christ.

I. WHAT DO YOU THINK OF THE DEITY OF JESUS CHRIST?

A. The Importance of His Deity.

1. *It is a foundation stone of the church.* The confession of our Lord's deity is the rock upon which God builds His church. If it were possible to take this away, the gates of hell would quickly prevail against the church.

2. *It is necessary to salvation.* If Jesus Christ is not God, I would never preach the gospel of Christ again. It would not be gospel. It would be only a system of moral ethics. It is the deity of our Lord that gives a sanction to His death and makes Him such a high priest as became us, who by the infinite merits of His suffering could fully satisfy an infinitely offended justice.

B. The Proof of His Deity.

1. *The testimony of inspired apostles.* We hear the apostle John pronouncing so positively that the Word (Jesus

Christ) was not only with God, but was God (John 1:1). Saint Paul also says that the Lord Jesus was in the form of God: that in Him dwelt "all the fulness of the godhead bodily" (Colossians 2:9).

2. *The testimony of Christ Himself.* Christ assumed the title which God the Father gave to Himself when He sent Moses to deliver His people Israel: "Before Abraham was, I am" (Exodus 3:14; John 8:58). And again, "I and My Father are one." It is evident that the Jews understood our Lord when He spoke thus as making Himself equal with the Father; otherwise, why did they stone Him as a blasphemer (John 10:30-33)?

II. WHAT DO YOU THINK OF THE MANHOOD OF JESUS CHRIST?

A. The Reason for the Incarnation.

1. *Man's present condition is not his original state.* It was God who made us. I would willingly think that no person is so blasphemous as to suppose. that since God made us, He made such creatures as we now find ourselves to be. This would be giving God's Word the lie, which tells us that "in the image of God (not the image which we now bear on our souls) made He man" (Genesis 1:27).

2. *Man's present condition is the result of sin.* God placed man in the Garden of Eden and condescended to enter into a covenant with him, promising eternal life upon the condition of obedience and threatening eternal death for disobedience. Man disobeyed, and acting as our representative involved both himself and us in the curse resulting from the fall. The reason why the Son of God took upon Him our nature was the fall.

B. The Purpose of the Incarnation.

1. *The eternal provision.* The eternal God, foreseeing how Satan would bruise the heel of man, had in His eternal counsel provided a means whereby He might bruise that accursed serpent's head. The Lord Jesus, the only begotten Son of God, offered to die to make an atonement for

man's transgression and to fulfill all righteousness in his stead.

2. *The fulfillment of the eternal provision.* Because it was impossible for Christ to die for our sins in that He was God and also since man had offended, it was necessary that atonement should be made in the person of man. Therefore, rather than that we should perish, Christ, the everlasting God, became man to fulfill the law and die for us in order to procure a union between God and our souls.

III. WHAT DO YOU THINK OF JUSTIFICATION THROUGH JESUS CHRIST?

A. False Views of Justification.

1. *Justification apart from Christ.* What do you think about being justified by Christ? I believe I can answer for some of you. Many, I fear, think to be justified, that is, looked upon as righteous in God's sight, without Jesus Christ. However, such will find themselves dreadfully mistaken: for out of Christ, "God is a consuming fire."

2. *Universal justification.* Others satisfy themselves with believing that Christ came into the world to save sinners in general; whereas their chief concern should be how they may be assured that Christ came to save them in particular. He "gave Himself for me" (Galatians 2:20). It is this immediate application of Christ to our own hearts that renders His merits effectual to our eternal salvation.

3. *Cooperative justification.* Others there are who go still further. They believe that Jesus Christ is the God-man. They hold that He is to be applied to their hearts and that they can be justified in God's sight only in and through Him. But they make Him only in part a Saviour because they are for doing what they can themselves and then Jesus Christ is to take up the deficiencies of their righteousness.

B. Scriptural Teaching on Justification.

1. *It is through faith.* We are justified through faith in Jesus Christ, without any regard to any work or fitness foreseen in us. All we have to do is to lay hold on His righteousness by faith. The very moment we apprehend it by a living faith, that moment we may be assured that the blood of Jesus Christ has cleansed us from all sin.

2. *It is gratuitous.* Salvation is the free gift of God. In the great work of man's redemption boasting is entirely excluded; which could not be if any one of our works were to be joined with the merits of Christ. Our salvation is all of God, from the beginning to the end. It is not of works, lest any man should boast; man has no hand in it (Ephesians 2:8-9).

CONCLUSION

This is glad tidings of great joy to all that feel themselves poor, lost, undone, condemned sinners. "Ho, every one that thirsteth, come unto the waters of life, and drink freely; come and buy, without money and without price" (Isaiah 55:1). Behold a fountain opened in your Savior's side for sin and for all uncleanness. "Look unto Him whom ye have pierced:" look unto Him by faith and you shall be saved.

14

Blind Bartimeus

> *And Jesus said unto him, Go thy way, thy faith hath made thee whole. And immediately he received his sight, and followed Jesus in the way.* — Mark 10:52

WHEN the apostle Peter was recommending Jesus of Nazareth in one of his sermons to the Jews, he gave Him a short, but withal a glorious and exalted character, "that He went about doing good." It was His meat and drink to do the works of Him who sent Him while the day of His public ministry lasted. He ministered to both the physical and spiritual needs. Sometimes the same person was the subject of both mercies. Such an example is Bartimeus (read Mark 10:46-52).

I. THE MAN'S NEED.

A. He Was Blind.

He had lost his sight. His case is still the more pitiful if he was, as some think his name indicates, the blind son of a blind father. Happy was it for Bartimeus that he could hear, though he could not see: for in all probability, upon hearing the noise and clamor of the people who followed our Lord, his curiosity led him to enquire about the cause of it.

B. He Was a Beggar.

Bartimeus, not being able to dig, begs for his living; and in order to make it a better trade, sat by the side of the highway — in all probability without or near the gate of the city where people must necessarily pass in and out.

II. THE MAN'S CRY.

A. It Was a Cry of Faith.

Although the eyes of his body were shut, yet the eyes of his mind were in some degree opened so that he saw, perhaps, more than most of the multitude that followed Jesus. As soon as he heard of it he began to cry out; which he would not have done had he not heard of Him before and believed that Christ was able and willing to restore sight to the blind.

B. It Was a Cry of Recognition of Jesus' Messiahship.

Bartimeus styles Him, "Jesus Thou Son of David." Thereby he gives evidence that he believed Him to be the Messiah who was to come into the world, unto whom the Lord God was to give the throne of His father David and of whose kingdom there was to be no end, of whom it had been long foretold (Isaiah 35) that when He should come "the eyes of the blind should be opened."

C. It Was a Cry of Confession of Need.

"He began to cry out." This implies that he had a deep sense of his own misery and the need of a cure. He began to cry out in order that Jesus might hear Him above the noise of the throng. He began to cry out as soon as he heard that Jesus was passing by, not knowing whether he might ever enjoy such an opportunity any more.

D. It Was a Cry for Mercy.

"Have mercy upon me," the natural language of a soul brought to lie down at the feet of a sovereign God. Here is no laying claim to a cure by way of merit; no proud self-righteousness; no bringing in a reckoning of performances, nor any doubting of Jesus' power or willingness to heal him. He speaks out of the abundance of his heart and in the language of the poor, broken-hearted publican, he cries out, "Jesus, Thou Son of David, have mercy on me."

III. THE EFFECT OF THE MAN'S CRY.

A. The Effect in Relation to the Crowd.

We would think that such a moving petition as Bartimeus' would have melted the whole multitude, but instead of that, we are told that "many charged him." The word in the original seems to imply a charge attended with threatening, and spoken in an angry manner. They charged him "to hold his peace." It may be that they threatened to beat him if he did not. They looked upon him as beneath the notice of Jesus.

B. The Effect in Relation to Jesus Christ.

1. *Jesus heard.* How does the Son of David treat the blind beggar? Does He join with the multitude and charge him to hold his peace? Does He go on, thinking him to be beneath His notice? No; for Mark relates: "And Jesus stood still." Although on a journey and in haste, it is not losing time to stop now and then to do a good deed by the way.

2. *Jesus called.* Jesus "commanded him to be called." Why so? To teach us to be condescending and kind even to poor beggars and tacitly to reprove the misguided zeal of the people who had charged Bartimeus to hold his peace. By this also our Lord prepares the multitude the better to take more notice of the blind man's faith and of His own mercy and power extended in the healing of him.

3. *Jesus healed.* In reply to Jesus' question, "What wilt thou that I should do unto thee?" blind Bartimeus requested sight for his blinded eyes. "Jesus said unto him, Go thy way, thy faith hath made thee whole. And immediately he received his sight." With the word there went a power; and He that spoke light out of darkness, saying, "Let there be light, and there was light," commanded light into this poor blind beggar's eyes and behold there was light. The miracle was instantaneous: immediately he received his sight.

CONCLUSION

How do you find your hearts affected at the relating of this notable miracle which Jesus wrought? Are you not ready to break out into the language of the song of Moses and to say, "Who is like unto Thee, O Lord, glorious in holiness, fearful in praises, continually doing wonders!" Come unto Him, all ye that are weary and heavy laden, and He will refresh you, He will give you rest. Be not afraid, you seek Jesus; behold He comes to meet you.

15

A Repentant Heart

> *Except ye repent, ye shall all likewise*
> *perish.* — Luke 3:3

W HEN we consider how heinous and aggravating our of-
fences are in the sight of a just and holy God, that they bring
down His wrath upon our heads and occasion us to live under His
indignation; how ought we thereby to be deterred from evil, or at
least, to repent thereof and not commit the same again. Repentance
denotes an abhorrence of evil and forsaking of it.

I. THE NATURE OF REPENTANCE.

A. It Is Sorrow for Sin.

Our sorrow and grief for sin must not spring merely from a
fear of wrath; for if we have no other ground than that, it pro-
ceeds from self-love and not from any love to God. If love to
God is not the chief motive of your repentance, your repentance is in vain and not to be considered true.

B. It Is Hatred of Sin.

It is not just your confessing yourselves to be sinners, it is not
merely knowing your condition to be sad and deplorable. This
is in vain so long as you continue in your sins. Your care and
endeavors should be to get the heart thoroughly affected there-
with, that you may feel yourselves to be lost and undone
creatures. If you are enabled to groan under the weight and
burden of your sins, then Christ will ease you and give you
rest.

C. It Is the Forsaking of Sin.

Resolve to leave all of your sinful lusts and pleasures. Abhor, renounce, forsake your old sinful course of life and serve God in holiness and righteousness the rest of your life. If you lament and bewail past sins and do not forsake them, your repentance is in vain; you are mocking God and deceiving your own soul. You must put off the old man with his deeds before you can put on the new man, Christ Jesus.

II. THE CAUSES OF REPENTANCE.

A. It Is God.

Now, as to the causes of repentance. The first cause is God. He is the Author, for "we are born of God" (John 1:13). God has begotten us, even God, the Father of our Lord Jesus Christ. It is He that stirs up to will and to do of His own good pleasure.

B. It Is God's Grace.

Another cause of repentance is God's free grace; it is owing to "the riches of His grace" (Ephesians 2:7), my brethren, that we have been prevented from going down to hell long ago; it is because the compassions of the Lord fail not, they are new every morning and fresh every evening.

C. It May be Through the Instrumentality of a Saint of God.

Sometimes the instruments are very unlikely. A poor despised minister or other member of the body of Christ may, by the power of God, be made the means in His hands of bringing men to true evangelical repentance. This may be done to show that the power is not in men, but that it is entirely owing to the good pleasure of God.

III. THE NECESSITY FOR REPENTANCE.

A. Because Man Is a Sinner.

Since we have sinned it is necessary to repent. A holy God could not, nor ever can, or will, admit anything that is unholy into His presence. There must be a change in heart and life before there can be a dwelling with God. No unclean person can stand in the presence of God; it is contrary to the holiness of His nature. There is a contrariety between the holy nature of God and the unholy nature of carnal and unregenerate men.

B. Because There Can Be No Communication Between God and the Sinner.

What communication can there be between a sinless God and creatures full of sin; between a God of purity and impure creatures? If you were to be admitted into heaven in your inpenitent condition, heaven would be a hell to you; the songs of angels would be intolerable to you. Therefore you must be changed, you must be holy as God is holy (I Peter 1:15-16). He must be your God on earth and you must be His people or you will never dwell together throughout eternity.

C. Because a Sinner Cannot Be Admitted into Heaven.

Singing praises to Him who sits upon the throne and to the Lamb is the employment of all who are admitted into heaven where neither sin nor sinner is allowed to enter, where no scoffer can come without repentance from his evil ways. This must be done before anyone can enter the glorious mansions of God which are prepared for all who love the Lord Jesus Christ in sincerity and truth.

IV. THE EXHORTATION CONCERNING REPENTANCE.

A. The Exhortation Addressed to Sinners.

There is no hope of any who live and die in their sins. They will dwell with demons and lost souls throughout all eternity. Consider, therefore, while you are going on in a course of sin and unrighteousness, the consequence that will attend your thus misspending your precious time. It is worth your while to be concerned about your souls. Will it not be deplorable when your good things on earth are past and your unconcern about eternity will gnaw at your soul?

B. The Exhortation Addressed to Believers.

Be thankful to God for His mercies towards you. Be thankful for this unspeakable mercy. As your life was formerly devoted to sin and the pleasures of this world, let it now be spent wholly in the ways of God. Let Christ's love to you keep you humble. Do not be high minded, keep close to the Lord. Let the love of Jesus be in your thoughts continually. His love for you is unfathomable.

CONCLUSION

Come and behold Christ crucified for you; see His hands and feet nailed to the cross. Come and see His pierced side. There is a fountain open for sin and for uncleanness. Come and see His head crowned with thorns. Can you think of a bleeding, dying Savior and not be filled with pity? He underwent all this for you. Come to Him by faith; there is mercy for every soul that will come to Him.

16

A Scriptural View of Self-denial

> *And He said unto them all, if any man*
> *will come after Me, let him deny himself.*
> — Luke 9:23

W HOEVER READS the gospel sincerely will find that our Lord took all opportunities of reminding His disciples that His kingdom was not of this world. He reminded them that His doctrine was a doctrine of the cross and that their profession of being His followers would call them to a constant state of voluntary suffering and self-denial.

I. THE NATURE OF SELF-DENIAL.

A. It Must Extend to Our Understanding.

We must not lean to our own understanding, but we must submit our short-sighted reason to the light of divine revelation. There are mysteries in Christianity which are above, but not contrary to our natural reason. We must in all humility and reverence embrace the truths revealed in the Scriptures; thus only can we become truly wise, even "wise unto salvation."

B. It Must Extend to Our Wills.

We must deny our wills, that is, we must not make our wills a principle of action. Do not imagine that we have no pleasure in anything we do — "wisdom's ways are ways of pleasantness"; but pleasing ourselves must be only the subordinate end of our actions. As we must renounce our wills in doing, so likewise we must renounce them in suffering, the will of God.

71

Whatever befalls us we must say, "Father not my will, but Thine be done."

C. It Must Extend to Our Affections.

We must deny ourselves the pleasurable indulgence and self-enjoyment of riches. We must look upon ourselves as stewards and not proprietors of the manifold gifts of God. We must renounce our affection for relatives when they stand in opposition to our love of and duty to God. We must deny ourselves the things that are indifferent in themselves, that is, the things lawful, but not expedient; for the immoderate use of them is harmful.

D. It Must Extend to Our Own Righteousness.

We must renounce our own righteousness. If we should give all our goods to feed the poor and our bodies to be burned, yet, if we in the least depend on that and do not wholly rely on the perfect all-sufficient righteousness of Jesus Christ, it will profit us nothing. "Christ is the end of the law for righteousness to every one that believeth." We are complete in Him.

II. THE UNIVERSAL OBLIGATION OF SELF-DENIAL

A. A Wrong Concept of the Obligation of Self-denial.

Too many, unwilling to take Christ's easy yoke upon them, in order to evade the force of the gospel precepts would pretend that all the commands concerning self-denial and the renunciation of self and the world belonged to our Lord's first and immediate followers and not to us and our children. Such persons greatly err, not knowing the Scriptures nor the power of godliness in their life.

B. The True Concept of the Obligation of Self-denial.

The teaching of Christ, like Himself, never changes. All the commands which we have in the epistles about mortifying our members which are upon the earth, of setting our affection on things above, and of not being conformed to this world; these are but so many incontestable proofs that the same holiness, heavenly-mindedness, and deadness to the world is as necessary for us as for our Lord's immediate followers.

III. THE REASONABLENESS OF SELF-DENIAL.

A. Illustrated in the Old Testament.

Naaman's servants said, when he refused to wash in the Jordan, "If the prophet had bid thee do some great thing, wouldst thou not have done it? How much rather then, when he saith to thee, wash and be clean?" If Christ had bid you do some difficult thing, would you not do it? Much more should you do it when He only bids you to deny what is harmful.

B. Illustrated in the New Testament.

When Peter was released from prison, had he hugged his chains and begged to have them replaced around his hands, would that not have revealed his love for slavery? Does not the person who refuses to deny himself act inconsistently? If we do not gird up the loins of our mind and follow Christ, are we not still in love with bondage?

IV. THE ENCOURAGEMENTS FOR THE PRACTICE OF SELF-DENIAL.

A. The Life of Christ.

Follow Christ from His cradle to the cross and see what a self-denying life He led! Do you think that He suffered everything in order to have us excused and exempted from sufferings? Far be it from any Christian to judge after this manner. Peter tells us, "He suffered for us, leaving us an example, that we should follow His steps."

B. The Lives of Godly Men.

Think often on the lives of the apostles, prophets, and martyrs who lived holy, self-denying, blameless lives. If self-denial was necessary for them, why not for us also? Are we not men of like passion with them? Do wo not live in the same wicked world as they did? Have we not the same Spirit to assist, support, and purify us as they did?

C. The Pains of Hell.

Think often on the pains of hell. Consider whether it is not better to cut off a right hand or foot and pluck out a right eye if they cause us to sin "rather than to be cast into hell, where the worm dieth not, and the fire is not quenched." Think how many thousands are now reserved with lost spirits unto the day of judgment. This must be our case shortly unless we deny ourselves and follow Jesus.

D. The Joys of Heaven.

Meditate on the joys of heaven. Think with what unspeakable glory those happy souls are now encircled who on earth were called to deny themselves as well as we, and were not disobedient to that call. Lift up your hearts frequently towards the mansions of eternal bliss and with an eye of faith see the Son of Man with His retinue of departed saints solacing themselves in eternal joys.

CONCLUSION

Let us believe on the Lord Jesus Christ and deny ourselves! By this alone, every saint that ever lived ascended into the joy of the Lord. We also shall soon be lifted up into the same blissful regions, there to enjoy eternal rest with the people of God, singing doxologies and songs of praise to the adorable Trinity.

17

The Most Needful Thing

But one thing is needful.　　— Luke 10:42

Iт was a characteristic of our blessed Redeemer to go about doing good. This motive brought Him to the house of His friend Lazarus at Bethany. Mary, the sister of Lazarus, seated herself at the feet of Jesus in a posture of a disciple. Martha, "cumbered with much serving," complained about Mary to Jesus. He answered her with these words, "Martha, Martha, thou art careful and troubled about many things, but one thing is needful; and Mary has chosen that good part, which shall not be taken away from her."

1. THE IMPORT OF THE WORDS OF THE TEXT.

A. The Meaning Stated.

Now, in a few words, the one thing needful is the care of the soul, opposed as you see in the text to the excessive care of body, about which Martha was gently admonished by our Lord. This is a general answer and it comprehends a variety of important particulars which is the business of our ministry often to open to you at large.

B. The Implications Suggested.

1. *The care of the soul implies a readiness to hear the words of Christ,* to receive both the law and the gospel from His mouth.

2. *It supposes that we learn from this divine Teacher the worth of our souls, their danger, and the remedy.*

75

3. *It assumes the sincere dedication of ourselves to the service of God* and a faithful adherence to it, notwithstanding all oppositions arising from inward corruptions or outward temptations.

C. The Scriptural Terms Enumerated.

This one thing needful is represented in various Scriptures by various names. Sometimes it is called "regeneration" or "the new creature,"[1] because it is the blessed work of God's efficacious grace. Sometimes it is termed the "fear of God" and sometimes "His love, and the keeping of His commandments"; and very frequently in the New Testament it is called "faith" or "receiving Christ and believing on Him," which therefore is represented as the "great work of God."

II. THE INTENTION OF THE WORDS OF THE TEXT.

A. To Show that It Is of Universal Concern.

Our Lord, you see, speaks of this "one thing" as needful in the general sense. He says not, for this or that particular person or for those of such an age, station, or circumstance in life, but needful for all. And indeed, when discoursing on such a subject, one might properly introduce it with these solemn words of the Psalmist, "Give ear, all ye people, hear, all ye inhabitants of the earth, both high and low, rich and poor together" (Psalm 49:1-2).

B. To Show that It Is of Highest Consequence.

As Solomon says of wisdom, that it "is more precious than rubies: and all the things thou canst desire are not to be compared unto her" (Proverbs 3:15), so I may properly say of this great and most important branch of wisdom, namely soul care. Whatever can be laid in the balance with it will be found lighter than vanity. This is strongly implied when it is said in the text, "one thing is needful"; one thing, and one thing alone is so.

---

1. Greek: new creation (Ed.)

C. To Show that It Is of a Comprehensive Nature.

The care of the soul is of so comprehensive a nature that everything truly worthy of our concern may be considered as included in it or subservient to it.   As David observes that "the commandment of God is exceeding broad" (Psalm 119:96), so we may say of this one thing needful. Solomon also, very justly and emphatically expresses it, "to fear God and to keep His commandments is the whole duty of man" (Ecclesiastes 12:13).

III. THE IMPORTANCE OF THE WORDS OF THE TEXT.

A. The Testimony of the Godhead.

In the Proverbs God speaks of those who neglect Him and their souls as fools, while the godly alone are designated as wise. If we enquire what our Lord judged to be needed most, the words of the text contain as full an answer as can be imagined; and the sense is repeated in Matthew 26:26.

B. The Testimony of Men.

The wisest and best men of all ages have agreed in this point, that this has been the unanimous judgment, this the common and most solicitous care, of those characters who are most valuable, to secure the salvation of their own souls and to promote the salvation of others.

C. The Testimony of the Evident Reason of the Case.

1. *The care of the soul is the one thing needful because without it you cannot secure peace of mind nor avoid the upbraiding of conscience.*

2. *It is necessary because happiness depends upon it.*
3. *It is needful in order to avoid a state of eternal misery.*

IV. THE IMPRESSIONS FROM THE WORDS OF THE TEXT.

A. Reason to Lament Man's Folly of Neglect.

Since the care of the soul is true wisdom, then surely we have reason to say with Solomon that madness is in men's hearts

(Ecclesiastes 9:3). Look on the conduct of mankind in general and you will imagine that they consider it the one thing needless, the vainest dream, and the most idle amusement of the mind. Can we, my Christian brethren, behold such a scene with indifference? The Lord awaken our compassion, our prayers, and our endeavors to bring them to Christ.

B. Necessity for Serious Inquiry.

Let me entreat you to remember your own concern in it and enquire: Have I thought seriously of it? Have I seen the importance of it? Has it lain with an abiding weight on my mind? Has it brought me to Christ, that I might lay the stress of these eternal interests on Him? Am I willing to give up other things, my interests, my pleasures, my desires, to this? Am I conversing with God and with man as one who believes these things?

CONCLUSION

May this care be awakened in those by whom it has been neglected! May it be revived in each of our minds. In order that you may be encouraged to pursue it with greater cheerfulness, let me conclude with this comfortable thought: in proportion to the necessity of the case through the merits of Jesus Christ is the provision which grace has made for our assistance. If you are disposed to sit down at Christ's feet, He will teach you by His Word and Spirit.

18

The Pharisee and the Publican

> *I tell you, this man went down to his house justified rather than the other: For everyone that exalteth himself, shall be abased; and he that humbleth himself, shall be exalted.* — **Luke 18:14**

In almost all of our Lord's discourses He preached the gospel to poor sinners and denounced terrible woes against proud selfjustifiers. The parable to which the words of the text belong (read the entire parable, Luke 18:10:14) includes both. The evangelist informs us that our Lord "spake it into certain ones who trusted in themselves, that they were righteous, and despised others." It is a parable worthy of your most serious attention.

I. THE TWO MEN IN THE PARABLE.

A. They Differ in Reputation.

1. *The Pharisee was a respected hypocrite.* The Pharisees were very zealous for the traditions of the fathers and for the observation of the rites and ceremonies of Judaism. For these reasons they were highly venerated by the people. They had such a reputation for piety among the Jews that it was said if there were but two men saved, one of them must be a Pharisee.

2. *The publican was a hated sinner.* The publicans were gatherers of the Roman taxes and amassed much wealth by falsely wronging men. They were so universally infamous that our Lord tells His disciples that the excommunicated man should be to them as a publican. The

Pharisees thought it a sufficient impeachment of our Lord's character that He was their friend and ate with them.

B. They Agree in the Duty of Public Worship.

1. *The evidence of the agreement.* They both came up to the temple. We have very early notice of men's sacrificing to and calling upon the Lord's name in the Old Testament. And it is nowhere contradicted in the New. Our Lord and His apostles went to the temple: and we are commanded by the Apostle: "not to forsake the assembling of ourselves together, as the manner of some is."

2. *The importance of public worship.* Although our devotions begin in our closets, they must not end there. If people do not enter into public devotions, I must suspect that they have little or none at home. The two men of the parable came to the temple, says our Lord, to pray. Thither should the children of God go up, to walk with and pour out their hearts before the mighty God of Jacob.

II. THE TWO PRAYERS OF THE PARABLE.

A. The Pharisee's Prayer.

1. *It was a relating of his works.* The Pharisee came to the temple to boast rather than to pray. He makes no confession of guilt or request for pardon of past sins or for grace to help assist him for the time to come. He only recounts his performances to God. This no one can justly do, that is, glory in His presence.

2. *It was a revealing of his self-righteousness.* If all of his boasted righteousness were true, he still could be a child of the devil. There is no mention made of his loving the Lord his God with all of his heart or a single syllable of inward religion. It is only an outward piety at the best; inwardly he is full of pride, self-justification, and great uncharitableness.

B. The Publican's Prayer.

    1. *It was a prayer of confession.* God be merciful to me a sinner by birth, a sinner in thought, word, and deed; a sinner as to my person, a sinner as to all of my performances; a sinner in whom is no health, in whom dwelleth no good thing; a sinner full of wounds and bruises and putrifying sores from the crown of the head to the sole of the feet.

    2. *It revealed his self-abasement.* Methinks I see him standing afar off, pensive, oppressed, and even overwhelmed with sorrow. And to show that his heart was full of self-resentment and that he sorrowed after a godly sort, he smote upon his breast. The word in the original implies that he struck hard upon his breast. He will lay the blame upon none but his own wicked heart.

III. THE TWO RESULTS IN THE PARABLE.

A. In Relation to the Two Men.

    1. *The Pharisee was not justified.* Let Pharisees take heed that they do not pervert this text: for when it is said, "This man went down to his house justified rather than the other," our Lord does not mean that both were justified, and that the publican had more justification than the Pharisee. That the Pharisee was not justified is certain, for God resisteth the proud.

    2. *The publican was justified.* A broken and a contrite heart God will not despise. I tell you, says our Lord, I who am God and therefore know all things, I who can neither deceive nor be deceived, whose judgment is according to right; I tell you this publican, this despised, sinful, but broken-hearted man, went down to his house justified (acquitted and looked upon as righteous in the sight of God) rather than the other.

B. In Relation to Its Teaching.

    1. *The self-righteous will be abased.* Every one without exception, young or old, high or low, rich or poor, who exalts himself; everyone who trusts in himself and rests in

his duties, or thinks to join them with the righteousness of Christ for justification in God's sight; he shall be abased in the sight of all good men, angels, and God Himself. He shall be abased to live with demons in hell forever more.

2. *The self-abased will be exalted.* He that humbles himself through grace, whatever he be, shall be exalted. He shall be exalted in a spiritual sense. He shall be freely justified from all of his sins through the blood of Christ. He shall have peace with God and joy in believing. He shall be indwelt by Christ. He shall drink of the divine pleasures as out of a river. He shall be brought into the presence of God.

CONCLUSION

One act of true faith in Christ justifies you forever. He is able to exalt you. God has exalted and given Him a name above every name, that at the name of Jesus every knee shall bow; nay, God has exalted Him to be not only a Prince, but a Savior. May He be a Savior to you.

19

The Conversion of Zaccheus

> *And Jesus said unto him, This day is sal-*
> *vation come to this house, forasmuch as he*
> *also is a son of Abraham. For the Son of*
> *Man is come to seek and to save that*
> *which was lost.* — Luke 19:9-10

Salvation, throughout Scripture, is said to be a free gift
of God through Jesus Christ our Lord. Not only free because God
is a sovereign agent and therefore may withhold it from or confer
it upon whom He pleases; but free because there is nothing to be
found in man that can in any way induce God to be merciful unto
him. The righteousness of Jesus Christ is the sole cause of our
finding favor in God's sight. (Read Luke 19:1-10.)

I. THE OBSTACLES TO ZACCHEUS' CONVERSION
verse 2.

A. He Was a Tax Gatherer.

Surely, no one will say that there was any fitness in Zaccheus
for salvation. He was a publican and therefore, in all probability a sinner. Publicans were gatherers of the Roman taxes
and were infamous for their abominable extortion. Zaccheus
being chief among the publicans consequently was chief among
the sinners.

B. He Was Rich.

One inspired apostle has told us that "not many mighty, not
many noble are called" (I Corinthians 1:26). Another says,
"God hath chosen the poor of this world rich in faith" (James

2:5). The Lord Jesus assures us that "it is easier for a camel to go through a needle's eye than for a rich man to enter into the kingdom of God" (Luke 18:25).

II. THE DETERMINATION OF ZACCHEUS
verses 3-4.

A. To See Jesus.

Rich as he was, we are told that "he sought to see Jesus." Our Lord's fame was now spread abroad throughout all Jerusalem and all the country round about. Some said that He was a good man and others, a deceiver. Therefore curiosity drew out this rich publican to see who this person was of whom he had heard such conflicting accounts.

B. To Overcome the Hindrances to Seeing Jesus.

Zaccheus, finding that he could not see Christ because of the crowd and the littleness of his stature, did not smite on his breast and depart saying, "It is in vain to seek after a sight of Him any longer, I can never attain to it." No, finding he could not see Christ if he continued in the midst of the crowd, he ran before the multitude and climbed up a sycamore tree to see Him.

III. THE LORD JESUS' INVITATION TO ZACCHEUS
verse 5.

A. The Friendliness of the Invitation.

Christ calls Zaccheus by name, as though He were well acquainted with him. Indeed, well might He so think; for the tax-gatherer's name was written in the book of life. He was one of those whom the Father had given to Him from all eternity. "For whom He did predestinate, them He also called" (Romans 8:30).

B. The Substance of the Invitation.

Amazing love! Well might Luke usher in the account with "behold." It is worthy of our admiration. When Zaccheus thought of no such thing, nay, thought Christ did not know him; behold the Lord Jesus does what we never hear He did before or after, I mean, invite Himself to Zaccheus' house. It was not, Pray let Me abide, but: I must abide this day at thy house.

IV. THE RESPONSE OF ZACCHEUS TO JESUS' INVITATION — verses 6-8.

A. He Received Christ.

With this outward call there went an efficacious power from God which overruled Zaccheus' natural will. Therefore, "He made haste, and came down, and received Him joyfully" (verse 6); not only into his house but also into his heart. Thus it is that the great God brings home His children. He calls them by name, by His Word or providence. He speaks to them also by His Spirit.

B. He Confessed Christ.

Zaccheus, having believed on Jesus in his heart, now makes confession of Him with his mouth. He "stood forth" (verse 8). He was not ashamed before his fellow publicans. True faith casts out all sinful fear of man. Again, he said, "Behold Lord" (verse 8). It is remarkable how readily people in Scripture have owned the deity of Christ immediately upon conversion.

V. THE FRUITS OF ZACCHEUS' SALVATION verse 8.

A. Charity.

"Behold the half of my goods I give to the poor." Not some small amount, but the half. Of what? My goods; things that were vauable. I give; not, I will give when I die, but I give them now. To whom would he give? Not to the rich, but to the poor, the maimed, the halt, the blind.

B. Restitution.

However, knowing that he must be just before he could be charitable, and conscious that in his public administrations he had wronged many persons, he adds, "If I have taken anything from any man by false accusation, I restore him four-fold." I suppose, before his conversion, he thought it no harm to cheat; but now he is grieved for it at his heart.

VI. THE ASSURANCE OF SALVATION GIVEN TO ZACCHEUS — verses 9-10.

A. Christ's Statement that Salvation Has Come to Zaccheus' House.

B. Christ's Statement that Zaccheus Is Now a True Son of Abraham.

He is a true son of Abraham not so much by a natural, as by a spiritual birth. He was made partaker of like precious faith with Abraham. Like Abraham he believed on the Lord and it was accounted to Him for righteousness. His faith, like Abraham's, worked by love; and I doubt not that he has been long since sitting in Abraham's harbor.

CONCLUSION

"For the Son of Man is come to seek and to save that which was lost" (verse 10). These words were spoken by our Savior in answer to some self-righteous Pharisees, who, instead of rejoicing with the angels in heaven at the conversion of such a sinner as Zaccheus, murmured "that He was gone to be guest with a man that is a sinner" (verse 7). To vindicate His conduct, He tells them that this was an act agreeable to the design of His coming.

20

The Marriage at Cana

*This beginning of miracles did Jesus in
Cana of Galilee, and manifested forth His
glory; and His disciples believed on Him.*
— John 2:11

THE CHIEF END that the apostle John had in view when
He wrote the gospel was to prove the deity of Jesus Christ against
those archheretics, the Ebionites and Cerinthians, whose perni-
cious principles too many follow in these last days. For this reason
John is more particular than any other evangelist in relating our
Lord's divine discourses and also the glorious miracles which He
wrought, not by the power derived from another, but from a power
inherent in Himself.

I. THE CIRCUMSTANCES OF THE MIRACLE.

A. It Was a Feast.

By our Lord's being at a feast we may learn that feasting upon solemn occasions is not unlawful. The Son of Man, we
know, "came eating and drinking." If a Pharisee asked Him
to come to his house our Lord went and sat down with him.
Then, we find, His conversation was always such as tended
toward edification. We may then, no doubt, go and do likewise.

B. It Was a Marriage Feast.

1. *Christ's presence sanctions marriage.* Our Lord graced a
   marriage feast with His first public miracle. It was an
   institution of God Himself, even in paradise; and therefore

lawful for all Christians, even for those who are made perfect in holiness through the faith of Jesus Christ.

2. *Christ should be consulted in every marriage.* We may learn the reason why we have so many unhappy marriages in the world. It is because the parties concerned do not call Jesus Christ by prayer. Christ and the Scriptures are the last things that are consulted.

C. It Was an Unusual Marriage Feast.

1. *Mary's request.* The persons who called our Lord and His disciples to the marriage feast seem not to have been rich. They had an insufficient quantity of wine. It was Mary who said to the Lord, "They have no wine." Herein she set an example to rich and poor. The rich should be willing to go into the cottages of the poor and consider their needs. The poor who are disabled from helping can pray for one another.

2. *Jesus' response.* The Lord's answer to Mary gives us reason to think that there was something which was not right. He said to her, "Woman, what have I to do with thee?" (verse 4). Will the Lord Jesus entirely disregard His mother's request? No; He intimates that He will do at the proper time the thing she desired of Him. "Mine hour is not yet come." As though He said, "When they are come to an extremity and sensible of the need of My assistance, then I will show forth My glory."

II. THE PURPOSES OF THE MIRACLE.

A. To Prove the Deity of Christ.

One of the purposes of this miracle the evangelist mentions in the text, "to show forth His glory," or to give a proof of His eternal power and godhead. This was the chief design of our Lord's turning water into wine. However, there are more which our Lord may be supposed to have had in view, some of which I shall proceed to mention.

B. To Reward the Host.

He might do this to reward the host for calling Him and His disciples to the marriage. Those who honor the Lord He will honor. A cup of cold water given in the name of a disciple shall in no wise lose its reward. Although those who abound in almsdeeds out of a true faith in and a love for Jesus Christ may seem, as it were, to throw their bread upon the waters, yet they shall find it again after many days.

C. To Signify the Outpouring of the Holy Spirit.

Our Lord's turning the water, which was poured out so plentifully, into wine is a sign of the pouring out of His Spirit into the hearts of believers. The Holy Spirit is in Scripture compared to wine. Therefore the prophet calls us to buy wine (Isaiah 55:1), that is, the Spirit of love who fills and gladdens the soul as it were with new wine. The Apostle alludes to this when he bids the Ephesians "not to be drunk with wine, wherein is excess, but be filled with the Spirit" (5:18).

D. To Reveal the Glory of the Latter Days.

1. *The work of God during past and present time.* Great things God has done already. Great things God is doing now. Many righteous men have desired to see the things which we see and have not seen them.

2. *The greater work of God in the future.* Glorious things are spoken of the times when "the earth shall be full of the knowledge of the Lord as the waters cover the sea" (Isaiah 11:9). All the former glory shall be nothing in comparison of that glory which shall excel.

E. To Show the Happiness of the Heavenly State.

1. *Present blessings.* The rewards which Christ confers on His faithful servants and the comforts of His love wherewith He comforts them while pilgrims on the earth are often so exceeding great that, if it were not promised, it would be almost presumption to hope for any reward hereafter. Nevertheless, my brethren, all the manifestations of God that we can possibly be favored with here,

when compared with the glory that is to be revealed in us, are no more than a drop of water when compared with the ocean.

2. *Future glory.* This corruptible is to put on incorruption; this mortal is to put on immortality. When God shall cause all His glory to pass before us then we shall cry out, "Lord, Thou hast kept Thy good wine until now. We have drunk deeply of Thy Spirit; we have heard glorious things of Thy city, O God! but now we find that not half, not the thousandth part has been told us."

CONCLUSION

I have spoken of the miracle for the same purpose for which He at first performed it, that is, "to show forth His glory," that you also may be brought to believe on Him. "Behold the Lamb of God who taketh away the sins of the world" (John 1:29). Look unto Him and be saved. May God give to all of you a hearing ear and an obedient heart.

21

Searching the Scripture

Search the Scriptures. — John 5:39

W HEN the Sadducees came to our Lord and put to Him the question of whose wife that woman should be in the next life, who had seven husbands in this; He told them that they erred, not knowing the Scriptures. If we would know whence all the errors that have overspread the church of Christ first arose, we should find that in a great measure they flowed from the same fountain, ignorance of God's Word. Our Lord, although He was the eternal God, yet as man, He made the Scriptures His constant rule and guide.

I. THE DUTY TO SEARCH THE SCRIPTURES.

A. Because They Reveal How All Mankind Died in Adam.

By the Scriptures, I understand all the books which have been accounted canonical and which make up that volume commonly called the Bible. Had man continued in a state of innocence he would not have needed an outward revelation because the law of God was written in his heart. Among other things, the Scriptures show us our misery, our fall, or in a word, after what manner we died in Adam.

B. Because They Reveal How All Men May Be Made Alive in Christ.

The Scriptures show us not only our fall in Adam, but also the necessity of the new birth in Christ Jesus. Hence then arises the need of searching the Scriptures. Since they are nothing else but the grand charter of our salvation, the revelation of a covenant made by God with men in Christ, and a light to guide us in the way of peace; it follows that all are charged to read and search them, because all are equally fallen from God, all equally stand in need of being informed how they must be restored to and united with Him.

II. THE DIRECTIONS FOR SEARCHING THE SCRIPTURES.

A. Remember the Chief End of the Scriptures.

Have always in view the end for which the Scriptures were written, namely, to show us the way of salvation by Jesus Christ. "Search the Scriptures," says our blessed Lord, "for they are they that testify of Me." Look, therefore, always for Christ in the Scriptures. In the Old Testament you will find Him under prophecies, types, sacrifices, and shadows; in the New He is manifested in the flesh to become a propitiation for our sins as a priest, and as a prophet to reveal the whole will of His heavenly Father. Have Christ always in view when you read God's Word.

B. Search the Scriptures with a Humble Disposition.

Whosoever does not read the Scriptures with a humble child-like disposition shall in no wise enter into a knowledge of the things contained in them. God hides the sense of them from those that are wise and prudent in their own eyes; He reveals them only to babes in Christ, who think they know nothing yet as they ought to know; who hunger and thirst after righteousness and humbly desire to be fed with the sincere milk of the Word in order that they might grow thereby. Be as willing to learn what God shall teach you as Samuel was when he said, "Speak, Lord, for Thy servant heareth."

C. Search the Scriptures with a Sincere Intention to Obey Them.

Search the Scriptures with a sincere intention to put into practice what you read. A desire to do the will of God is the only way to know it. If any man will do God's will, says Christ, "he shall know of the doctrine, whether it be of God, or whether I speak of Myself." Again, speaking to His disciples, He says, "to you (who are willing to practice the Word) it is given to know the mysteries of the kingdom of God, but those who are without (who do not practice the Word) all these things are spoken in parables" that they may not see nor understand.

D. Apply the Scriptures to Yourself.

In order to search the Scriptures still more effectively, make an application of everything you read to your own lives. Whatever was written in the Book of God was written for our learning. What Christ said unto those aforetime, we must look upon as spoken to us also. Since the Holy Scriptures are nothing but a revelation from God, how fallen man is to be restored by Jesus Christ, all the precepts, threats, and promises belong to us and to our children, as well as to those to whom they were immediately made known.

E. Seek the Direction of the Holy Spirit.

The natural man does not discern the words of the Spirit of God because they are spiritually discerned. The words which Christ has spoken, they are spirit and they are life. They can be no more understood as to the true sense and meaning of them by the mere natural man than a person who never had learned a language can understand another speaking in it. It was the lack of the assistance of the Holy Spirit that made Nicodemus, a teacher of Israel, so utterly ignorant concerning the doctrine of regeneration.

F. Pray Immediately Before Searching the Scriptures.

Let me advise you to pray before you read the Scriptures. Intersperse short ejaculatory prayers while you are engaged in reading. Pray over every word and verse, if possible, and when you close the Book most earnestly beseech God that the words which you have read may be engrafted into your hearts and bring forth in you the fruits of a good life. It will cause the Scriptures to enlighten, quicken, and enflame your soul.

G. Constantly Search the Scriptures.

"Search the Scriptures," that is, dig in them as for hidden treasure.   Here is a manifest allusion to those who dig in mines; and our Saviour would thereby teach us that we must take as much pains in constantly reading His Word, if we would grow wise thereby, as those who dig for silver or gold. Search the Scriptures daily.

CONCLUSION

Taste and see how good the Word of God is, and then you will never leave it to feed on the dry husks, those trifling sinful compositions in which men of false taste delight themselves. You will then disdain such poor entertainment and blush that you once were fond of it.   The Word of God will then be sweeter to you than honey and the honey-comb, and dearer than gold and silver.   Your souls, by reading it, will be filled, as it were, with marrow and fatness.

22

The Killing Sin —
The Rejection of Christ

*And ye will not come to Me, that ye may
have life.* — John 5:40

Our Lord says to the religious teachers of Israel, "Ye
will not come to Me, that ye may have life" — I am now present
with you, I am now come to explain the Scriptures and fulfill
them, I am now come to proclaim to you that life, that eternal life,
which the Scriptures declare was to be proclaimed by Me, yet "Ye
will not come." God knows this is the treatment Jesus Christ meets
with even today.

I. THE IMPLICATION OF THE CONDITION OF THE SINNER.

A. He Is Legally Dead.

The text supposes that we are all dead in sin, for if we are
not, why do we need to come to have life? Sin is transgression
of the law. Every transgression of the law incurs damnation.
Have we eaten of the forbidden fruit? We must die. We are
legally dead. We have broken God's law. We are liable to
eternal condemnation. We are therefore legally dead, every
one of us without distinction or exception.

B. He Is Spiritually Dead.

Besides legal death, there is spiritual death. By the latter is
meant that the sinner is deprived of that life of God in which
he originally stood. The consequence of this is eternal death.

95

If a man dies physically when he is in the state of spiritual death he must die forever, by which is meant that he must live eternally banished from God.

II. THE REVELATION OF THE PROVISION FOR THE SINNER.

A. Legal Life.

"Ye will not come to Me, that ye may have life." What life is this? If ever a sinner possesses life he must be acquitted, he must be pronounced not guilty. His conscience says guilty, but Jesus Christ came that he might have legal life, that he might be acquitted from all that condemnation which he is under because of the breaking of God's law.

B. Spiritual Life.

Since man through sin has lost the divine image which was his original dignity, he will never reach glory without the restoration of that image. Spiritual life in the heart comes from Jesus Christ and this is the life of God in the soul of man. This is not something metaphorical, but it is a real thing. Death came through Adam, but life comes through Jesus Christ.

III. THE IMPLICATION OF THE MANNER OF THE SALVATION OF THE SINNER.

A. What It Is.

The only way to get this life is to come to Jesus Christ. Our text says, "Ye will not come unto Me, that ye may have life"; implying that without coming to Him man cannot have life. "There is no other name under heaven given among men whereby we must be saved" (Acts 4:12). "I am the way, the truth, and the life" (John 14:6). In order to have this life we must come to Christ for it.

B. What It Does Not Mean.

1. *It does not mean coming to see His person.* It can never mean this. Our Lord talks of coming to Him when He Himself was the preacher and they were all around Him.

Although so many were around Him, yet there was only one who touched Him.

2. *It does not mean coming to the ordinances and church services.* Thousands come to the ordinances and do not see the God of the ordinances in them. Thousands go to church and do not come to Christ.

C. What It Does Mean.

We must come to Christ to be acquitted, to be pardoned. We must believe on Him not only with a speculative belief, but we must have His blood applied and brought home to the soul. We must come to Him as the author and finisher of our faith. We must come to Jesus Christ and believe on Him for life eternal.

IV. THE EXPLANATION FOR THE REJECTION OF SALVATION BY THE SINNER.

A. Because He Does Not Think He Is Dead.

Why will not people come to Christ to have life? Because they do not think that they are dead and therefore they do not want salvation. They do not see themselves as fallen creatures. Remember when you say you are "rich and increased in goods" that you know not, says Christ, that "you are poor and miserable and blind and naked" (Revelation 3:17).

B. Because He Is Self-righteous.

Men do not choose to come to Christ because they do not chose to have Him as a free gift. They do not like to come to Him as poor and needy. The lawyers and other Jews thought they were righteous and therefore they would not come to Jesus Christ. Our Lord spoke of the Pharisees who trusted in themselves that they were righteous and would not come to Him that they might have life.

C. Because He Loves the World.

You will not come to Him because you love the world. "If any man love the world, the love of the Father is not in Him"

(I John 2:15). When I talk of loving the world, I mean an inordinate love. I may live in the world and live upon it; yet my heart may be towards God. The love of the world is to be renounced and therefore men will not come to the Lord Jesus, they think, until they are going out of the world.

D. Because He Hates Christ.

If you are one of those who hate Christ, why you are the man that will not come to Him. "Why," you say, "does anybody hate Christ?" Everyone of us by nature hates Him. We hate Christ because He is despised, we hate Him because of the appearance of the people that are His followers, we hate Him because of the narrowness of the way we are to pass in to Him, we hate Him because we must part from our lusts.

CONCLUSION

As the Lord lives, in whose name I speak, if you will not come to Christ to have life you must come to His bar to hear Him pronounce you damned to all eternity. If you come to Him that you may have life, "Come ye blessed" will be the gracious welcome; but if you refuse, "Depart ye cursed" will be your sentence from the Lord. "For yet a little while, and He that shall come will come, and will not tarry" (Hebrews 10:37).

23

The Indwelling of the Holy Spirit

> *In the last day, that great day of the feast,*
> *Jesus stood, and cried, saying, If any man*
> *thirst, let him come unto Me and drink.*
> *He that believeth on Me, as the Scripture*
> *hath said, out of his belly shall flow rivers*
> *of living water. But this spake He of the*
> *Spirit, which they that believe on Him*
> *should receive.* —John 7:37-39

OUR LORD attended the temple service in general and the Jewish festivals in particular. The festival at which He was now present was that of the Feast of Tabernacles, which the Jews observed according to God's appointment in commemoration of their living in tents. At the last day of this feast it was customary for many pious people to fetch water from a certain place and bring it on their heads singing the anthem, "And with joy shall ye draw water out of the wells of salvation" (Isaiah 12:3). Our Lord observing this cries out the words found in the text. The inspired evangelist adds the explanatory words (verse 39a) which are the basis of the present discourse.

I. THE PERSON OF THE SPIRIT.

A. He Is the Holy Spirit.

By the Spirit is evidently to be understood the Holy Spirit.

B. He Is Deity.

He is the third person in the ever-blessed Trinity, consubstantial and co-eternal with the Father and the Son, proceeding from, yet equal to them both. Our Lord, when He gave His apostles the commission to go and teach all nations, commanded them to baptize in the name of the Holy Spirit, as well as the Father and the Son. Peter in Acts 5:3 said to Ananias, "Why hath Satan filled thine heart to lie unto the Holy Ghost?" and in verse 4 he says, "Thou hast not lied unto men, but unto God." From these passages it is plain that the Holy Spirit is truly and properly God.

II. THE POSSESSION OF THE SPIRIT.

A. The Persons Possessing the Spirit.

Unless men have eyes which see not and ears that hear not, how can they read the latter part of the text and not confess that the Holy Spirit is the common privilege of all believers, even to the end of the world? "This spake He of the Spirit, which they that believe on Him should receive." Observe, He does not say, they that believe on Him during one or two ages, but they that believe on Him at all times and in all places. So we must believe that even we also shall receive the Holy Spirit if we believe on the Lord Jesus with our whole hearts.

B. The Significance of Possessing the Spirit.

Our Lord, just before His bitter passion, prayed that all of His true followers might be united to Him by His Holy Spirit, by as real, vital, and mystical an union as there was between Jesus Christ and the Father (John 17:21-23). I say all of His true followers; for it is evident from our Lord's own words that He had us and all true believers in view when He prayed this prayer (John 17:20). Unless we treat our Lord as the high priests did, and count Him a blasphemer, we must confess that all who believe in Jesus Christ through the Word or ministration of His servants are to be joined to Jesus Christ by being made partakers of the Holy Spirit.

III. THE REASONABLENESS OF THE DOCTRINE OF THE INDWELLING OF THE SPIRIT.

A. Man's Natural Condition.

However this doctrine of the indwelling Spirit may seem foolishness to the natural man, yet to those who have tasted the good Word of life and have felt the power of the world to come, it will appear to be founded on the highest reason; and is capable to those who have eyes to see, of a demonstration — because it stands on this self-evident truth that we are fallen creatures. Do we not find that by nature we are prone to pride? Do we not find in ourselves the seeds of malice, revenge and all uncharitableness? Do we not by nature follow and suffer ourselves to be led by our natural appetites? We are no better than those whom Jude calls brute beasts (verse 10).

B. Man's Need in Order to Dwell with God and to Enjoy Him.

Since it is true that we are all by nature, since the fall, a mixture of brute and devil, it is evident that we all must receive the Holy Spirit before we can dwell with and enjoy God. We, as well as the apostles, must receive the Spirit of God. For the great work of sanctification, or making us holy, is particularly referred to the Holy Spirit; therefore, our Lord said, "Except a man be born . . . of the Spirit, he cannot enter into the kingdom of God" (John 3:5). However often we have told God we believe in the Holy Spirit, yet, if we have not believed in Him, so as to be united to Jesus Christ by Him, we have no more concord with the Lord Jesus than Belial himself.

CONCLUSION

Notwithstanding you are sunk into the nature of the beast and devil, yet, if you truly believe on Jesus Christ you shall receive the quickening promised in the text and be restored to the glorious liberty of the sons of God. "For by grace are ye saved through faith; and that not of yourselves: it is the gift of God: not of works, lest any man should boast" (Ephesians 2:8-9). Come then, my guilty brethren, come and believe on the Lord that bought you with His precious blood; look up by faith and see Him whom ye pierced. Behold Him with arms stretched out to receive you; cry unto Him as did the penitent thief. He will be to you wisdom, righteousness, sanctification and eternal redemption.

24

The Good Shepherd

My sheep hear My voice, and I know
them, and they follow Me: and I give unto
them eternal life; and they shall never
perish, neither shall any man pluck them
out of My hand. — John 10:27-28

W E ARE TOLD that our Lord was at Jerusalem at the Feast
of Dedication and it was winter. This feast was held in commemoration of the restoration of the temple and altar after its pro-
fanation by Antiochus Epiphanes. "He walked in the temple in
Solomon's porch." The Jews surround Him and endeavor to
catch Him by a question. After aswering the question He speaks
the words of the text.

I. THE GOOD SHEPHERD'S SHEEP.

A. Their Description.

1. *They love to be together.* There are only two kinds of people mentioned in Scripture. Christ divides the whole
   world into two classes: sheep and goats. Believers are always compared to something good and profitable and un-
   believers are always described by something that is bad.
   Sheep generally love to be together. We speak of a flock
   of sheep, we do not say a herd of sheep.

2. *They are small, harmless, and quiet.* Sheep are little creatures, and Christ's people may be called sheep because they
   are small in the eyes of the world and they are even less
   in their own eyes. Sheep are looked upon as the most
   harmless and quiet creatures that God has made. May

God give us to know that we are his sheep by having this blessed temper infused into our hearts by the Holy Spirit.

3. *They easily stray and are lost.* Of all creatures, sheep are the most apt to stray and be lost. Christ's people may in this respect be compared to sheep. Turn out a horse or a dog and they will find their way home, but a sheep wanders about. Thus Christ's sheep are too apt to wander from the fold; having their eyes off the great Shepherd they go into this field and that field, over this ledge and that ledge.

4. *They are useful.* Sheep are the most useful creatures in the world. They cloth our bodies with wool, and there is not the least part of a sheep but is useful to man. May God grant that you and I may, in this respect, answer the character of sheep. We should labor with our hands that we may have to give to all those in need.

B. Their Ownership.

1. *They are given to the Shepherd.* Believers consider Christ's property in them; He says, "My sheep." Oh, blessed be God for that little, yet great word "My." We are His by eternal election: "the sheep which Thou hast given Me," says Christ. They were given by God the Father to Christ Jesus in the covenant made between the Father and the Son from all eternity.

2. *They were purchased by the Shepherd.* I want to lead you to Calvary, there to see at what expense of blood Christ purchased those whom He calls His own. He redeemed them with His own blood, so that they are not only His by eternal election, but also by actual redemption in time. They were given to him by the Father upon condition that He should redeem them by his heart's blood.

3. *They voluntarily surrender to the Shepherd.* They are His because they are enabled in a day of God's power voluntarily to give themselves up unto Him. Christ says of these sheep especially that they hear His voice and that they follow Him. Here is an allusion to a shepherd. In the eastern nations the shepherds generally went before,

they held up their crook, and they had a particular call that the sheep understood.

II. THE GOOD SHEPHERD'S ASSURANCE TO HIS SHEEP.

A. He Knows His Sheep.

1. *He knows their number and name.* If you belong to Jesus Christ, He is speaking of you when He says, "I know My sheep." What does this mean? Why, He knows their number, He knows their names, He knows every one for whom He died; and if there were to be one missing for whom Christ died, God the Father would send Him down again from heaven to fetch Him. "Of all (saith He) that Thou hast given Me I have lost none."

2. *He knows all about them.* Christ knows His sheep. He not only knows their number and name, but the words speak the peculiar knowledge and notice He takes of them. He takes as much care of them as if there were only one single sheep in the world. He knows His saints. He is acquainted with all of their sorrows, trials, and temptations. He bottles up their tears. He knows their inward corruptions. He knows all their wanderings and He takes care to bring them back again.

B. He Keeps His Sheep.

1. *They shall never perish.* Christ says, I have brought them out of the world to Myself and do you think that I will let them go to hell after that? "I give to them eternal life"; pray, mind that: not I will, but I do. Some speak of being justified at the day of judgment. That is nonsense. If we are not justified here, we shall not be justified there. He gives them eternal life, that is, assurance of it; the indwelling of the Spirit of God here is the earnest of the glory hereafter.

2. *They shall never be plucked out of the Shepherd's hand.* He holds them by His power, none shall pluck them thence. There is always something plucking at Christ's sheep. The devil, the lusts of the flesh, the lusts of the eye, and

the pride of life, all try to pluck them out of Christ's hand
We help all three to pluck themselves out of Jesus' hand;
but "none shall pluck them out of My hand," says Christ.
Upon that text I can leave all of Christ's sheep to the protection of His love.

CONCLUSION

If you never were among Christ's sheep before, may He bring
you now. Come, see what it is to have eternal life. Do not refuse
it. May the great, good Shepherd draw your souls. If you have
never heard His voice before, God grant you may hear it now.
And you, dear Christian, who are already in His hands, may God
keep you from wandering and keep you near Christ's feet.

25

The Convicting Work of the Holy Spirit

And when He is come, He will reprove
the world of sin, and of righteousness, and
of judgment.   — John 16:8

T HESE WORDS contain part of a gracious promise which
the Lord Jesus made to His sorrowing disciples. The person referred to in the words of the text is plainly the Holy Spirit. The
promise was first made to our Lord's apostles and fulfilled on
the day of Pentecost. Nevertheless, as the apostles were the
representatives of the whole body of believers, we must infer that
this promise must be looked upon as spoken to us and to as many
as the Lord our God shall call.

I. THE HOLY SPIRIT CONVICTS THE WORLD OF SIN.

The word which we translate *reprove* ought to be rendered
convince. In the original it implies a conviction by way of
argumentation and coming with a power upon the mind equal
to a demonstration.

A. He Convicts the Sinner of Sin in the Life.

The Holy Spirit generally convinces of some enormous sin,
the worst perhaps of which the convicted person was ever
guilty. Thus our Lord dealt with the persecutor Saul. He
convinced him first of the horrid sin of persecution. Such a
sense of all his other sins probably at the one time revived in
his mind that he immediately died to all his false confidences.

B. He Convicts the Sinner of Sin in the Nature.

When the Holy Spirit accosts a sinner and convinces him of sin, all carnal reasoning against original sin is immediately thrown down; and he is made to cry out, "Who shall deliver me from the body of this death?" Now he does not so much bewail his actual sins as the inward perverseness of his heart which he finds to be in direct enmity against God.

C. He Convicts the Sinner of the Sin of Legal Righteousness.

We are by nature legalists, thinking to be justified by the works of the Law. When somewhat awakened by the terrors of the Lord, we immediately go about to establish our own righteousness by works and think thereby to find acceptance with God. The Comforter convinces the soul of these false notions and makes the sinner to see that all his righteousnesses are as filthy rags.

D. He Convicts the Sinner of the Sin of Unbelief.

There is a fourth sin of which the Comforter convinces the soul and which alone our Lord mentions (verse 9), as though it were the only sin worth mentioning. Indeed it is the root of all other sins. It is the reigning as well as the condemning sin of the world. It is the cursed sin of unbelief.

II. THE HOLY SPIRIT CONVICTS THE WORLD OF RIGHTEOUSNESS.

A. The Meaning of Righteousness.

By the word *righteousness,* in some places of Scripture, we are to understand that common justice which we ought to practice between man and man. However, in our text (as in a multitude of other places in Holy Writ) it refers to the active and passive obedience of our Lord; it is that perfect, personal, all-sufficient righteousness which He has wrought out for the world of which the Spirit is to convince.

B. An Evidence of the Righteousness of Christ.

"Of righteousness," says our Lord, "because I go to the Father, and ye see Me no more" (verse 10). This is one argument which the Holy Spirit uses to prove Christ's righteousness: because He is gone to the Father and we see Him no more. Had He not wrought out a sufficient righteousness, the Father would have sent Him back as not having done what He undertook.

C. The Importance of the Holy Spirit's Work of Convicting of Righteousness.

Whoever knows himself and God must acknowledge that Jesus Christ is the end of the Law for righteousness to every one that believes and that we are to be made the righteousness of God in Him. Whatever other scheme of salvation men may lay, I acknowledge I can see no other foundation whereon to build my hopes of salvation but the rock of Christ's personal righteousness imputed to my soul.

D. The Reason for the Holy Spirit's Work of Convicting of Righteousness.

Many, I believe, have a rational conviction that salvation depends on the imputation of Christ's personal righteousness to the soul; but rational convictions, if rested in, avail but little. It must be a spiritual, experimental conviction of saving truth. Therefore our Lord says that when the Holy Spirit comes He convinces of that righteousness; of its reality, completeness, and sufficiency to save a poor sinner.

III. THE HOLY SPIRIT CONVICTS THE WORLD OF JUDGMENT.

A. The Explanation of Judgment

The next thing of which the Comforter, when He comes, convinces the soul is judgment. By the word *judgment* I understand that well-grounded peace, that settled judgment, which the soul forms of itself when it is enabled by the Spirit of God to lay hold on Christ's righteousness, which I believe it always does when convinced of righteousness.

B. The Significance of the Conviction of Judgment.

The soul being enabled to hold on Christ's perfect righteousness by a living faith has a conviction wrought in it by
the Holy Spirit that the Prince of this world is judged. The
soul now being justified by faith has peace with God through
our Lord Jesus Christ. The strong man armed is now cast
out; my soul has true peace; the Prince of this world will come
and accuse, but he has now no share in me.

C. The Confidence of the Conviction of Judgment.

The blessed Spirit which I have received and whereby I am
enabled to apply Christ's righteousness to my poor soul, powerfully convinces me of this: Why should I fear or of what shall
I be afraid, since He, the Spirit of God, witnesses with my
spirit that I am a child of God? Such an one can triumphantly
say, It is Christ that justifies me, who is he that condemns?

CONCLUSION

Thank God for His gift of the Holy Spirit. You would never
have been thus highly favored had not He who first spoke darkness into light loved you with an everlasting love and enlightened
you by His Holy Spirit, and that too, not on account of any good
thing foreseen in you, but for His own name's sake. Be humble
and extol free grace. Walk as it becomes the children of light.
And, oh, that the Holy Spirit would come and convince the Christless of sin, righteousness, and judgment.

26

Conversion

> *Repent ye, therefore, and be converted,*
> *that your sins may be blotted out, when*
> *the times of refreshing shall come from*
> *the presence of the Lord.*
>
> **— Acts 3:19**

Peter charged his audience with the sin of murdering the Son of God. No doubt the charge entered deep into their conscience and that faithful monitor began to give them a proper sense of themselves. Then the Apostle informed them that great as was their sin, it was not unpardonable; that although they had been connected with the crime of murdering the Lord and thereby incurred the penalty of eternal death, yet there was mercy for them as pointed out in the text.

I. MEN'S CONCEPTS OF CONVERSION.

I shall endeavor to show you what conversion is not. I believe there are thousands that think themselves converted, and yet at the same time, if you come and examine them, they know not so much as speculatively what real conversion is.

A. Some Think Conversion Is Only a Change from one Religious System to Another.

There is a notion that a person's change from one church or denomination to another is conversion. This may take place while no thought is given to Jesus Christ. This is conversion only from one persuasion to another persuasion.

111

B. Some Think Conversion Is Only a Change from one Doctrinal Position to Another.

Possibly a person may go further and be converted from one set of principles or doctrines to another. Neither is this real or Scriptural conversion, that is, conversion that will bring a soul to heaven.

C. Some Think Conversion Is Only Reformation.

Some think they are converted because they are reformed; but reformation is not renovation. A man may be turned from profanity to a regard for morality, and because he does not swear nor attend the theater nor play cards he considers himself converted; yet he may still be unsaved. I speak not against reformation or being good. This is right in its place; but this conversion, or the two previously mentioned, you may have and yet never be truly converted.

II. SCRIPTURAL VIEW OF CONVERSION.

A. Its Meaning.

A man must be a new creature and be converted from his own righteousness to the righteousness of the Lord Jesus Christ. As a child when born has all the several parts of a man, so when a person is converted to God there are all the features of the new creature and growth until he become mature in grace and is taken to glory. Anything short of this is but the shadow instead of the substance. Conversion means a person turned from hell to heaven, from the world to God.

B. Its Evidence.

They that are really converted to Jesus and are justified by faith in the Son of God, such will take care to evidence their conversion by grace diffusing itself through every faculty of the soul and making a universal change in them. He that is "in Christ is a new creature: old things (not will be, but) are passed away; behold, all things (not only will, but) are become new" (II Corinthians 5:17).

C. Its Author.

The author of this conversion is the Holy Spirit. It is not man's free will; it is not moral persuasion; nothing short of the influence of the Spirit of the living God can effect this change in our lives. We are said to be born of the Spirit (John 3:5). "That which is born of the flesh is flesh; and that which is born of the Spirit is spirit" (John 3:6).

III. MOTIVES FOR CONVERSION.

A. Conversion Is Necessary for Soul Rest.

Permit me to say that you ought to repent and be converted, for until then you never can, never will, never shall find true rest for your souls.

B. Conversion Is Necessary for Eternal Happiness.

Unless you are converted you can never be happy hereafter. You must be converted if you will go to heaven. The unconverted man would not enjoy heaven, if he could enter, which, of course, he cannot.

C. Conversion Is Necessary for Deliverance from Condemnation.

I mention one more thing, which is, that you must be converted or be damned. This is plain English, but not plainer than my Master made use of when He said, "He that believeth not shall be damned" (Mark 16:16).

IV. ANSWERS TO OBJECTIONS AGAINST CONVERSION.

A. There Is Still Sufficient Time to be Converted.

The common saying is, "I do not care to be converted yet; I think there is time enough to be converted." You may think to put it off until the morning, but before morning you may be damned. If you were in prison and you would be permitted to leave, you would choose to go immediately. Why will you not do for your soul what you would do for your body?

B. People Will Laugh.

I would be converted but people will laugh at me. Suppose you were promised $50,000, but you must be laughed at all your life time. Would you accept the offer? There is none but would say, "Give me the $50,000." If you loved God and your souls you would say, "Give me God and call me what you will." Is the gospel the glory of our country and are you ashamed of the Gospel?

C. It Is Not the Right Time.

Is it time for the poor prisoners to be converted, who are to be hanged tomorrow morning? If it is time for them, it is time for you, for you may be dead before them. There was a poor woman who a few days ago was cursing most shockingly; now she is a dead corpse. God grant that may not be the case with you; but the only way to prevent it is to remember that "now is the accepted time; now is the day of salvation" (II Corinthians 6:2).

CONCLUSION

Young people, I charge you to consider. God help you to repent and be converted. You middle aged people, oh, that you would repent and be converted! You old, grey headed people, the Lord make you repent and be converted that you may thereby prove that your sins are blotted out. I could preach until I preached myself dead. I would be glad to preach myself dead if God would convert you. May God bless His work on you that you may blossom and bring forth fruits unto Him.

27

The Almost Christian

> *Almost thou persuadest me to be a Christian.* — Acts 26:28

T HE CHAPTER out of which the text is taken contains an account of Saint Paul's conversion to Christianity which he gave before governor Festus and king Agrippa. The king accuses the Apostle of madness to which he replies in the negative and confronts the ruler with the words, "believest thou the prophets? I know that thou believest them." The text is Agrippa's confession.

I. THE IDENTIFICATION OF THE ALMOST CHRISTIAN.

A. He Wavers Between Christ and the World.

An almost Christian, if we consider him in his duty God-ward, is one that halts between two opinions; that wavers between Christ and the world; that would reconcile God and mammon, light and darkness, Christ and Belial. He is one who depends much upon outward form and therefore considers himself righteous, despising others; but at the same time he is a stranger to the divine life.

B. He Is Just to All.

If you consider him in respect to his neighbor, he is one who is strictly just to all. This does not proceed from any love to God or regard to man, but only through a principle of self-love. He knows dishonesty will spoil his reputation and consequently hinder his thriving in the world.

C. He Depends on Negative Goodness.

He is one who depends upon being negatively good and contents himself with the consciousness of having done no one any harm; even though he reads in the gospel that "the unprofitable servant was cast into outer darkness" (Matthew 25:30) and the barren fig tree was cursed and dried up from the roots, not for bearing bad fruit, but because it bore no fruit (Matthew 21:19).

D. He Is Publicly Charitable.

He is no enemy to charitable contributions, if not approached too frequently; but he is unaquainted with the ministry of visiting the sick and imprisoned, clothing the naked, and relieving the hungry in a private manner. He thinks that those things belong only to the clergy, yet his own false heart tells him that nothing but pride keeps him from exercising these acts of humility.

E. He Practices Sobriety.

As he is strictly honest to his neighbor, so he is likewise strictly sober in himself. Both his honesty and sobriety proceed from the same principle of self-love. It is true, he does not run into the same excesses of riot with other men, but it is not out of obedience to God, but because he is naturally temperate or is fearful of forfeiting his reputation or unfitting him for business.

II. THE REASONS FOR BEING AN ALMOST CHRISTIAN.

A. False Ideals of Christianity.

Many who live in a Christian country do not know what Christianity is. Some consider that it is found in this or that communion, others think it is morality, many more hold it to be a round of performance of duties. Only a few acknowledge it to be what it is in reality, a divine life, a union of a soul with God.

B. Fear of Man.

A second reason that so many are only almost Christians is a servile fear of man. There are many who have been awakened to a sense of the divine life, yet out of a sinful fear of being considered peculiar they have suffered all of these good impressions to wear off. They love man's praise more than the honor which God gives.

C. Love of Money.

This was the pitiable case of the young man in the gospel who enquired of our Lord what to do to inherit salvation, but went away sorrowful because he refused to part with his wealth (Luke 18:18-23). Thus many today when they find that they must forsake all to follow Christ say, "The Lord pardon us in this thing! We pray Thee have us excused."

D. Love of Pleasure.

Neither is the love of pleasure a less uncommon or less fatal cause why so many are no more than almost Christians. They have too great a love for pleasures. Tell them to "mortify their members" (Colossians 3:5) and they consider it as difficult as to cut off a right hand or to pluck out a right eye. They cannot think our Lord requires so much.

E. Instability of Character.

Many a minister and sincere Christian has wept over promising converts who seemingly began in the Spirit, but after a while fell away and ended in the flesh through an instability and fickleness of character. Christianity was to them a novelty, something which pleased them for a short time, but after their curiosity was satisfied they laid it aside.

III. THE FOLLY OF BEING AN ALMOST CHRISTIAN

A. It Is Not Salvation.

The first proof I shall give of the folly of being an almost Christian is that it is ineffectual to salvation. It is true that such men are almost good; but almost to hit the mark is really to miss it. God requires us to love Him with all our hearts, with all our souls, and with all our strength (Matthew 22:37). He loves us too well to admit any rival.

B. It Is Detrimental to Others.

An almost Christian is one of the most harmful creatures in the
world. He is a wolf in sheep's clothing. He is one of those
false prophets our Lord bids us beware, who would persuade
men the way to heaven is broader than it really is and thereby
"enter not into the kingdom of God themselves; and those who
are entering in, they hinder."

C. It Is Ingratitude Toward Christ.

It is the greatest instance of ingratitude that we can express
towards our Lord and Master Jesus Christ. Did He not come
down from heaven and shed His precious blood to purchase
these lives of ours and shall we only give Him half of them?
How can we say we love Him when our hearts are not wholly
with Him?

CONCLUSION

Let us scorn all base and treacherous treatment of our King and
Savior, of our God and Creator. Let us not take some care to go
to heaven and yet be lost at last. Let us give God our whole hearts
and no longer halt between two opinions. If the world is god, let
us serve that; if pleasure is a god, let us serve that: but if the
Lord is God, let us serve Him alone.

28

The Believer's Blessings in Christ

*But of Him are ye in Christ Jesus, who of
God is made unto us, wisdom, righteous-
ness, sanctification, and redemption.*
— I Corinthians 1:30

Of all the verses in the Book of God, this which con-
stitutes our text is, I believe, one of the most comprehensive.
What glad tidings it brings to believers! What precious privileges
are believers herein invested! Without referring you to the context I shall from these words point out to you the Fountain from
which these blessings flow and then consider what these blessings
are, wisdom, righteousness, sanctification, and redemption.

I. THE FOUNTAIN OF THE BELIEVER'S BLESSINGS

A. It Is God the Father.

First, I point out to you the Fountain of the blessings that the
children of God partake of in Jesus, "who of God is made unto
us": the Father, He it is who is spoken of here.

B. It Is the Father's Covenant with His Son.

There was an eternal contract between the Father and the Son:
"I have made a covenant with My chosen, and I have sworn
unto David My servant" (Psalm 89:3). David was a type of
Christ with whom the Father also made a covenant that if He
would obey, suffer, and make Himself a sacrifice for sin He
"shall see His seed, He shall prolong His days and the pleasure
of the Lord shall posper in His hands" (Isaiah 3:10).

119

C. It Is the Father's Love.

The Apostle when here speaking of the Christian's blessings, lest they should sacrifice to their own worth or think that their salvation was owing to their own faithfulness or improvement of their own free will, reminds them to look back on the everlasting love of God the Father — "who of God is made unto us."

II. THE EXPLANATION OF THE BELIEVER'S BLESSINGS.

A. Christ the Believer's Wisdom.

1. *The meaning of true wisdom negatively stated.*

   a. It is not indulging the desires of the flesh: eat, drink, and be merry. This is only the wisdom of brutes.

   b. It is not the gaining of things: for riches often take wings and fly away. "A man's life consisteth not in the abundance of the things which he possesseth" (Luke 12:15).

   c. It is not the gaining of knowledge. It is possible for you to tell numbers of the stars and call them all by their names and yet be mere fools. Learned men are not always wise.

2. *The meaning of true wisdom positively stated.*

   a. It is to know oneself. One of the wise men of Greece said, "Know thyself." This is certainly true wisdom. It is the wisdom spoken of in the text. We are made to know ourselves so as not to think more highly than we ought to think.

   b. It is to know what we are by nature. Once we were in darkness, fallen creatures, dead in trespasses in the sins, sons and heirs of hell and children of wrath.

   c. It is to know what we are by grace. Now we are light in the Lord and know He is the only Savior and have received Him as our all in all.

B. Christ the Believer's Righteousness.

1. *This means the imputation of Christ's righteousness to the believer.* Christ's whole personal righteousness is made over to and accounted to the believer. God the Father blots out our transgressions as with a thick cloud; our sins and iniquities He remembers no more. We are made the righteousness of God in Christ Jesus, who is the end of Law for righteousness to every one who believeth (Romans 10:4).

2. *This means the believer's deliverance from the guilt of sin.* The believer is actually acquainted. Hence it is that the Apostle, under a sense of this blessed privilege, breaks out in this triumphant language, "It is Christ that justifies, who is he that condemns?" (Romans 8:33-34). Does sin condemn? Christ's righteousness delivers believers from the guilt of it. Christ is their Savior and the propitiation for their sins. Who shall lay anything to their charge?

C. Christ the Believer's Sanctification.

1. *Sanctification is the renovation of the whole man.* By sanctification I do not mean a hypocritical attendance on outward ordinances nor a mere outward reformation. By sanctification I mean a total renovation of the whole man. By the righteousness of Christ believers become legally alive, by sanctification they are made spiritually alive. By the one they are entitled to glory, by the other they are made ready for glory. They are sanctified therefore in spirit, soul, and body.

2. *Sanctification is the effect and evidence of justification.* Although sanctification is not the cause, yet it is the effect of our acceptance with God — "who of God is made unto us righteousness and sanctification." He therefore who is really in Christ is a new creation. To look into our lives and see that they are changed and renewed gives to us a comfortable and well grounded assurance of the safety of our states. By our fruits we must judge whether we have or do not have the Holy Spirit.

D. Christ the Believer's Redemption.

1. *Redemption's end.* It is the believer's glorification. Our text sufficiently proves the final perseverance of all true believers. God never justified a man whom He did not sanctify, nor sanctify one whom He did not completely redeem and glorify. As for God, His way and work is perfect. He always carries on and finishes the work He begins. Those whom God has justified, He has in effect glorified.

2. *Redemption's area.* By the word redemption we are to understand not only a complete deliverance from all evil, but also a full enjoyment of all good both in body and soul.

   a. Christ's resurrection was an earnest of our resurrection. As in Adam all die so all in Christ shall be made alive.

   b. The complete redemption of our souls will be in heaven when the very being of sin will be destroyed and an eternal stop will be put to inbred, indwelling corruption.

CONCLUSION

You see, brethren, partakers of the heavenly calling, what great blessings are treasured up for you in Jesus Christ and what you are entitled to by believing on His name. Take heed, therefore, that ye walk worthy of the vocation wherewith you are called. Think often how highly you are favored; and remember, you have not chosen Christ, but He has chosen you.

29

A Worthy Resolution

*I determined not to know anything among
you, save Jesus Christ, and Him crucified.*
— I Corinthians 2:2

THE PERSONS to whom these words were written were the
members of the Corinthian church. They were not only divided
into different sects, by one saying, "I am of Paul," and another, "I
am of Apollos," but also had many amongst them who were so
full of this world's wisdom and so wise in their own eyes that
they set at naught the simplicity of the gospel, and accounted the
Apostle's preaching foolishness. What was the sum of Paul's
wisdom? He tells them in the words of the text, which is a resolution worthy of the great apostle Paul and no less worthy for
every minister and every disciple of Christ.

I. THE CONTENT OF THE RESOLUTION.

A. A Determination to Know.

1. *Not just historical knowledge.* By the word know we are
   not to understand a bare historical knowledge; for to know
   only historically that Christ was crucified by His enemies
   at Jesusalem will do us no more good than to know that
   Caesar was slain by his friends at Rome.

2. *But to approve.* The word know means to know so as to
   approve; as when Christ said, "I know you not," that is, I
   know you not so as to approve you. It implies experimental knowledge.

B. A Determination to Know Jesus Christ Crucified.

By Jesus Christ we are to understand the eternal Son of God. He is called Jesus, Savior, because He saves us from the guilt and power of our sins. He is called Christ, which signifies anointed, because He was anointed by the Holy Spirit to be a prophet to instruct, a priest to make atonement, and a king to govern. He was crucified upon the cross that He might become a curse for us; for it is written, "Cursed is every man that hangeth upon a tree" (Galatians 3:13). This knowledge so gripped the Apostle that he was determined not to know anything else. He resolved to make this the governing principle of his life.

II. THE REASONS FOR THE RESOLUTION.

A. Without Christ Crucified Our Persons Will Not Be Acceptable to God.

Christ is the way, the truth, and the life, and no one comes to the Father but through Him (John 14:6). He is the Lamb slain from the foundation of the world (Revelation 13:8). None ever were or ever will be received up into glory but by an experimental application of His merits to their hearts. We might as well think to rebuild the tower of Babel or reach heaven with our hands as to imagine we could enter therein by any other door than that of the knowledge of Jesus Christ. Other knowledge may make you wise in your own eyes and puff you up; but this alone edifies and makes wise unto salvation.

B. Without Christ Crucified Our Deeds Will Not Be Acceptable to God.

"Through faith," that is, through a living faith in a Mediator to come, "Abel offered a more acceptable sacrifice than Cain" (Hebrews 11:4). It is through a like faith, an experimental knowledge of the same divine Mediator, that our sacrifices of prayer, praise, and thanksgivings come up as an incense before the throne of grace. As our devotions to God will not, so neither, without this knowledge of Jesus Christ will our acts of charity to men be accepted by Him. If we gave all our goods

to feed the poor and yet were destitute of this knowledge, it
would profit us nothing.

C. Without Christ Crucified Our Morality Will Not Be Acceptable to God.

While we grant that morality is a substantial part of Christianity and that Christ came not to destroy or take away moral law
as a rule of action, but to explain and so fulfil it; yet we affirm
that our moral actions are not acceptable in the sight of God
the Father unless they proceed from the principle of a new
nature or a vital faith in the Son of God. Whether we eat or
drink or do anything for man, it must all be done out of a love
for and knowledge of Him who died and rose again. This is
necessary to render our works, even our most ordinary deeds,
acceptable in the sight of God.

III. THE PRACTICE OF THE RESOLUTION.

A. The Essential Thing in the Practice of the Resolution.

May I exhort you to put the Apostle's resolution into practice
and beseech you, with him, to determine "not to know anything, save Jesus Christ, and Him crucified." I say, determine,
for unless you sit down first and count the cost and from a
well grounded conviction of the excellency of this above all
other knowledge whatsoever, resolve to make this your chief
study, your only end, your one thing needful, every frivolous
temptation will draw you aside from the pursuit after it. The
more your enemies persuade you to know other things, the
more should you determine not to know anything but Christ
crucified.

B. The Importance of the Practice of the Resolution.

Riches shall fail, pomp shall cease, vanities shall fade away;
but the knowledge of Jesus Christ and Him crucified abides
forever. Of whatever, therefore, you are ignorant, do not be
ignorant of this. If you know Christ and Him crucified you
know enough to make you happy, although you know nothing
else; without this all of your other knowledge cannot keep you
from being everlastingly miserable. Do not value the contempt

of friends with which you must necessarily meet upon your open profession to act according to this determination. Your Master, whose you are, was despised before you.

CONCLUSION

Let us not be content with following Christ afar off, for then we shall, as Peter did, soon deny Him. Let our speech and all of our actions declare to the world whose disciples we are and that we have indeed determined not to know anything save Jesus Christ and Him crucified. Then it will be well with us and we shall be unspeakably happy here; and, what is infinitely better, when others that despised us shall be calling upon the mountains to be falling upon them, we shall be exalted to sit down on the right hand of God and shine as the sun in the firmament, in the kingdom of our Redeemer.

30

Temples of the Living God

Ye are the temples of the living God.
— **II Corinthians 6:16**

I F I MISTAKE NOT, the end proposed by the apostle Paul in the words of the text is to encourage believers to use all diligence to walk worthy of Him who called them. The expression, "Ye are the temple of the living God," undoubtedly is metaphorical, but under the metaphor something real and of infinite importance is to be understood. There seems to be an allusion not only to temples or churches in general, but to the Jewish temple in particular.

I. DEDICATION TO GOD.

A. In Relation to the Jewish Temple.

I trust but few, if any, need be informed that the preparations for the Jewish edifice were exceedingly grand, that is, it was modelled and built by a divine order and when completed it was separated from common uses and dedicated to the service of Jehovah with the utmost solemnity.

B. In Relation to Christians.

1. *The requirement.* Christians are the temple of the living God. Loved from eternity, effectually called in time, they are chosen out of the world and voluntarily devote themselves soul and body to the service of God. This is the Christian's reasonable service. It implies no less than the total renunciation of the world; in short, it turns the

Christian's entire life into one continued sacrifice of love to God; so that, whether he eats or drinks, he does all to God's glory.

2. *Its signification.* I would not insinuate that obedience to the words of the text requires us to become hermits. Christians are said to be the salt of the earth and the lights of the world and are commanded to "let their light shine before men." How can this be done if we shut ourselves up? True renunciation of the world is to be in the world but yet not of it; to have our hands employed on earth and our hearts at the same time fixed on things above.

II. DEVOTION TO GOD.

A. In Relation to the Jewish Temple.

The Jewish temple was a house of prayer. For this end was it built and adorned with such furniture. Solomon, in that admirable prayer which he offered to God at the dedication of the temple, said, "Hearken therefore unto the supplication of Thy servant, and of Thy people Israel which they shall make towards this place." What was said of the first, our Lord applies to the second temple, "My house shall be called a house of prayer."

B. In Relation to Christians.

1. *Its expression.* When believers are wholly dedicated to God their hearts become the seats of prayer from whence, as so many living altars, a perpetual sacrifice of prayer and praise is continually ascending up to the Father of mercies, the God of all consolations. Such, and such only, who thus worship God in the temple of their hearts, can truly be said to be made priests unto God or be styled a royal priesthood; such only can be styled "the temple of the living God." Devotion is expressed through prayer and praise.

2. *Its nature.* Let no one say that such a devotion is impracticable or practicable only to a few and those few being such as have nothing to do with the common affairs of life; for this is the common duty and privilege of all true Chris-

tians. To "pray without ceasing" and to "rejoice in the Lord always" are precepts equally obligatory on all who name the name of Christ. Such devotion, as expressed through prayer and praise should be habitual and universal among the children of God.

III. DWELLING OF GOD.

A. In Relation to the Jewish Temple.

The Jewish temple was also a place where the great Jehovah was pleased to reside. Hence, He is said to place and record His name there and to sit or dwell between the cherubims. When Solomon first dedicated it, we are told, "the house was filled with a cloud, so that the priests could not stand to minister by reason of the cloud, for the glory of the Lord had filled the house."

B. In Relation to Christians.

Wherefore all this manifestation of the divine glory in the Jewish temple? To show how the high and lofty One makes His abode in all those who tremble at His Word.

1. *The testimony of the inspired apostle Paul.* To this the Apostle more particularly alludes in the words immediately following our text; for having called the Corinthians "the temple of the living God," he adds, "as God hath said, I will dwell in them, and I will walk in them, and I will be their God, and they shall be My people." Strange and strong expressions are these words! Strange and strong as they are, they must be experienced by all who are indeed "the temple of the living God."

2. *The testimony of Christ.* The testimony of the apostle Paul declares nothing more or less than the prayer of our Lord which He prayed for His people a short time before His bitter passion, "that they may be one, even as we are one: I in them, and Thou in Me, that they may be made perfect in one." The truth of this glorious passage is not only for the apostles, but for all of God's children. The time would fail to mention all the Scriptures that speak of this blessing.

3. *The testimony of the church universal.* In asserting this doctrine we do not give utterance to the fancies of a disordered brain and uncontrolled imagination; neither do we broach any new doctrines or set up the peculiar opinions of any particular sect or denomination of Christians; but we speak the words of truth, we show you the right and good way, even that which all the articles of all the protestant churches and all sincere Christians, however differing in other aspects, do universally agree.

CONCLUSION

When Jehovah filled the temple with His glory, king Solomon burst forth into the pathetic exclamation, "Will God dwell with men on the earth?" With greater astonishment we ought to say, "Will the high and lofty One who inhabits eternity dwell in us?" Are you not ready to say, "Not unto us, but unto Thy free, unmerited, sovereign, distinguishing love and mercy, O Lord, be all the glory." We have nothing but what is freely given us from above.

31

The Power of Christ's Resurrection

That I may know Him, and the power of His resurrection.

— Philippians 3:10

T HE APOSTLE in the context cautions the Philippians to beware of the Judaizing teachers. And that they might not think he spoke out of prejudice or ignorance he acquaints them of his life as a Pharisee. However, when it pleased God to reveal His Son in him, the privileges he had formerly boasted in he counted "loss for Christ." He shows the sincerity of this conversion from Pharisaism when he says, "I count them but dung, so that I may win Christ, that I may know Him and the power of His resurrection.

I. THE FACT OF CHRIST'S RESURRECTION.

A. The Precautions to Prevent Dishonesty.

He was buried in a sepulcher hewn out of a rock, so that it could not be said that any digged under and conveyed Him away. It was a sepulcher wherein never man before was laid, so that if anybody did rise from thence, it must be the body of Jesus of Nazareth. Besides, the sepulcher was sealed; a great stone rolled over the mouth of it; and a band of soldiers (consisting not of friends, but of His professed enemies) was set to guard it.

B. The Post-resurrection Appearances of Christ.

Our blessed Lord's post-resurrection appearances at different times and various ways to His disciples, as when they were assembled together, when they were walking to Emmaus, when they were fishing; nay, and condescending to show them His hands and feet, and His appearing to over five hundred brethren at once, put the truth of His resurrection out of all dispute.

C. **The Qualification of the Writers of the Gospel Records.** They were eye witnesses of what they related; they ate and drank with Him after His resurrection. They were plain men, therefore less suspected of telling a lie, particularly since they laid down their lives for a testimony of the truth of it. The wonderful success God gave to their ministry when three thousand were converted by one sermon, and twelve poor fishermen in a very short time enabled to be more than conquerors over all the opposition of men or demons was a plain demonstration that Christ was risen.

II. THE NECESSITY FOR CHRIST'S RESURRECTION.

A. In Order to Fulfill Christ's Teaching.

Christ had often appealed to His resurrection as the most convincing proof He would give them that He was the true Messiah (Matthew 12:39-40). He also said, destroy this temple of My body, and in three days I will build it up (John 2:19-21). These words His enemies remembered and urged as an argument to induce Pilate to grant them a guard to prevent His being stolen from the grave (Matthew 27:63). Had He not risen again they might have justly said, "We know that this man was an imposter."

B. In Order to Give Believers Assurance of Salvation.

It had pleased the Father to wound His only Son for our transgressions and to confine Him in the grave as our surety for our guilt. Had Christ continued in the grave, we could have had no more assurance of salvation than any debtor can have of his creditor's satisfaction while his surety is kept confined. But by Christ being released from the power of death, we are thereby assured that with His sacrifice God was well pleased and that our atonement was finished upon the cross.

C. In Order to Give Assurance of the Resurrection of Our Bodies.

It was necessary that our Lord should rise again from the dead to assure us of the certainty of the resurrection of our bodies. The doctrine of the resurrection of the body was set at naught by the Gentiles, as appears from the Athenians' mockingly calling Paul a babbler and a setter forth of strange doctrines when he preached to them Jesus and the resurrection (Acts 17:18). Although it was believed by most of the Jews, nevertheless, the whole sect of the Sadducees denied it. But the resurrection of Jesus Christ put it out of dispute.

III. THE IMPORTANCE OF THE POWER OF CHRIST'S RESURRECTION.

A. The Explanation of the Power of the Resurrection.

It is to be raised from the death of sin to a life of righteousness and true holiness by the operation of the Holy Spirit. The resurrection of Christ's body Paul was satisfied would avail him nothing unless he experienced its power in raising his dead soul. One of the chief ends of our Lord's rising from the dead was to enter heaven as our representative and to send down the Holy Spirit to apply that redemption He had finished on the cross to our hearts by working an entire change in them.

B. The Appropriation of the Power of the Resurrection.

"He that liveth and believeth in Me shall live" (John 11:25). "By grace are ye saved through faith" (Ephesians 2:8). Believe and you shall live in Christ and Christ in you. By this faith we are not to understand a dead speculative faith, an intellectual faith only; but a living principle wrought in the heart by the powerful operation of the Holy Spirit, a faith that will enable us to overcome the world and forsake all in affection for Jesus Christ.

C. The Results of the Power of the Resurrection in the Life of the Believer.

Says the Apostle, "being made conformable to His death" (verse 11); thereby implying that we cannot know the power of Christ's resurrection unless we are made conformable to Him in His death. If we can reconcile light and darkness, heaven and hell, then we may hope to know the power of Christ's resurrection without dying to ourselves and the world. There is such an opposition between the spirit of this world and the spirit of Christ that he who will be at friendship with the one must be at enmity with the other.

CONCLUSION

Oh, the depth of the riches and excellency of Christianity! Well might the great apostle Paul count all things but dung and dross for the excellency of the knowledge of it. Well might he desire so ardently to know Jesus and the power of His resurrection. For even on this side of eternity it raises us above the world and makes us to sit in heavenly places in Christ Jesus. Oh, that we were all like-minded; that we felt the power of Christ's resurrection as the great company of worthies in Hebrews 11.

32

Intercession the Duty of Every Christian

Brethren, pray for us.

I Thessalonians 5:25

IF WE ENQUIRE why there is so little love amongst
Christians, we shall find our answer largely in the neglect or super-
ficial performance of intercessory prayer — imploring the divine
grace and mercy in the behalf of others. Some neglect this duty
because they seldom pray for themselves or are so selfish in their
prayers that they do not enlarge their petitions for the welfare of
their fellow Christians and others as they ought.

I. THE CHRISTIAN'S RESPONSIBILITY IN RELATION TO INTERCESSORY PRAYER.

A. The Universality of Prayer.

1. *It is present among all mankind.* Prayer is a duty founded
upon natural religion; the heathen never neglect it, although many Christian heathen amongst us do.

2. *It is an essential part of Christianity.* It is so essential to
Christianity that you might as reasonably expect to find a
living man without breath as a true Christian without the
spirit of prayer and supplication. In the heart of every
true believer there is a heavenly tendency which draws
him to converse with God.

B. The Reasons for Prayer.

1. *Personal.* A sense of their own weakness and of Christ's
fulness will not let them rest from crying day and night to

their Almighty Redeemer. Thus earnest and importunate are all sincere Christians in praying for themselves.

2. *Intercession.* Whereas, were the love of God shed abroad in our hearts and we loved our neighbor in the same manner that Christ loves us, we would be as importunate for their spiritual and temporal welfare as for our own.

II. THE SUBJECTS OF THE INTERCESSORY PRAYER

A. All Men.

"I exhort therefore," says the Apostle, "that first of all, supplications, prayers, intercessions, and giving of thanks be made for all men" (I Timothy 2:1). For as God's mercy is over all His works, as Christ died to redeem a people out of all nations; so we should pray that "all men may come to a knowledge of the truth, and be saved" (I Timothy 2:4).

B. Rulers of Nations.

Next to praying for all men we should pray for rulers, in order that we may lead quiet lives in all godliness and honesty (I Timothy 2:2). If we consider the heavy burden of government and how much the welfare of any people depends on the zeal and godly conduct of the rulers, the difficulties and temptations to which they are exposed, we shall not only pity but pray for them.

C. The Ministers of the Gospel.

You ought especially to pray for those whom "the Holy Spirit has made overseers over you." This is what the apostle Paul begs again and again of the churches to whom he writes. He says in the text, "Brethren, pray for us"; and again, in his epistle to the Ephesians, "praying always with all prayer and supplication for me, that I may open my mouth boldly, to make known the mystery of the gospel" (Ephesians 4:18-19).

D. Our Friends.

Our friends claim a place in our intercessions. We should not be content with praying in general terms for them, but we should suit our prayers to their particular circumstances. We have many instances in Scripture of the success of such intercessory prayer; but none more remarkable than that of Abraham's servant who prayed in a most particular manner in behalf of Isaac, and his intercession was answered (Genesis 24).

E. Our Enemies.

As we ought to intercede for our friends, so in like manner must we also pray for our enemies. "Bless them that curse you, and pray for them which despitefully use you, and persecute you" (Matthew 5:44). These commands the Lord Jesus were enforced in the strongest manner by His own example, as for instance, His prayer on the cross, "Father, forgive them, for they know not what they do" (Luke 23:34).

F. The Afflicted.

We should intercede for all who are afflicted in mind or body, for all who desire and stand in need of our prayers and for all who do not pray for themselves. And oh! that all believers would set apart some time every day for the due performance of this most necessary duty.

III THE INCENTIVES TO INTERCESSORY PRAYER.

A. It Will Increase Our Love to One Another.

He who daily intercedes at the throne of grace for all mankind will in a short time be filled with love and charity to all. Envy, malice, and such like hellish tempers can never long harbor in a gracious intercessor's breast; but he will be filled with joy, peace, meekness, longsuffering and all of the other graces of the Holy Spirit. He will rejoice with those who do rejoice and weep with those who weep.

B. It Is Efficacious.

Consider the many instances in Holy Scripture of the power and efficacy of intercessory prayer. It has stopped plagues, it has opened and shut heaven, and it has frequently turned away God's fury from His people. Abraham's intercession freed

Abimelech's house of the disease which God had sent amongst them. When Daniel interceded for the Lord's inheritance, how quickly was an angel dispatched to tell him that his prayer was heard.

C. It Is Probably the Frequent Employment of Glorified Saints.

Although the glorified saints are delivered from the burden of the flesh and restored to the glorious liberty of the sons of God, yet their happiness cannot be perfectly consummated until the resurrection. Therefore we cannot but think they are often importunate in beseeching our Heavenly Father shortly to accomplish the number of His elect and to hasten His kingdom. Shall not also we who are on earth be often exercised in this divine employ?

D. It Is the Unceasing Employment of the Glorified Christ.

To provoke you to this great work and labor of love, remember that it is the never ceasing employment of the holy and highly exalted Christ who sits at God's right hand to make continual intercession for us. So that he who is constantly employed in interceding for others is doing that on earth which the eternal Son of God is always doing in heaven.

CONCLUSION

And now brethren, what shall I say more, since you are taught of Jesus Christ to abound in love and in this good work of praying one for another. Although ever so humble and as poor as Lazarus, you will then become benefactors to all mankind; thousands and twenty times ten thousands will then be blessed for your sakes.

33

Persecution Every Christian's Lot

*Yea, and all that will live godly in Christ
Jesus, shall suffer persecution.*
— II Timothy 3:12

W HEN our Lord Jesus was pleased to take upon Himself
the form of a servant and go about preaching the kingdom of God,
He took all opportunities to forewarn His disciples of the many
distresses, afflictions, and persecutions they must expect to endure
for His name's sake. The apostle Paul, the author of this epistle,
following the steps of His Master, takes particular care to warn
young Timothy of the difficulties he must expect to meet with in
the course of his ministry.

I. THE MEANING OF LIVING GODLY IN CHRIST JESUS.

A. Such Persons Must Experience the New Birth.

To live godly in Christ Jesus supposes that we are made the
righteousness of God in Christ, that we are born again and are
made one with Christ by a living faith and a vital union even
as Christ and the Father are one. They that are in Christ are
new creatures; old things are passed away and all things are
become new in their hearts. Their life is hid with Christ in
God; their souls daily feed on the invisible realities of another
world.

B. Such Persons Must Submit to God's Will

To live godly in Christ is to make the divine the sole principle
of all our thoughts, words, and actions. Those who live godly

in Christ may not so much be said to live as Christ to live in them. They are led by His Spirit and are willing to follow the Lamb whithersoever He leads them. They hear, know, and obey His voice. They habitually live to God and daily walk with God.

II. THE CLASSIFICATIONS OF PERSECUTION TO WHICH THE GODLY ARE EXPOSED.

A. The Persecution of the Heart.

The Pharisees hated and persecuted our Lord long before they laid hold of Him: and He mentions being inwardly hated of men as one kind of persecution which His disciples were to undergo. This heart enmity is the root of all other kinds of persecution and is in some degree or other to be found in the soul of every unregenerate man. Many are guilty of this persecution who never have it in their power to persecute in any other way.

B. The Persecution of the Tongue.

Many, I suppose, think it no harm to shoot out arrows, even bitter words, against the disciples of the Lord. However they may esteem it, in God's account evil speaking is a high degree of persecution. Thus Ishmael's mocking Isaac in the Old Testament is termed persecuting him in the New Testament. It is a breach of the sixth commandment to slander any one; but to slander the disciples of Christ because they are His disciples must be highly provoking in God's sight.

C. The Persecution of Deeds.

The third and last kind of persecution is that which expresses itself in actions; as when wicked men separate the children of God from their company, or expose them to church censures, or threaten and prohibit them from making an open profession of Christianity, or interdict ministers for preaching the Word; or when they call them into courts; or when they fine, imprison, or punish them by confiscation of goods, scouring, or death.

III. THE REASON WHY THE GODLY MUST EXPECT PERSECUTION.

A. Because Our Lord Taught It.

Our Lord says, "Blessed are they which are persecuted for righteousness' sake: for theirs is the kingdom of heaven" (Matthew 5:10). We are not blessed with an interest in the kingdom of heaven unless we are or have been persecuted for righteousness' sake. Our Lord employs three verses in this beatitude and only one in each of the others; not only to show that men are unwilling to believe it, but also the necessary consequence of it upon our being Christians.

B. Because Our Lord Experienced It.

Follow Him from the manger to the cross and see whether any persecution was like that which the Son of God underwent while here on earth. How was he hated by wicked men! How was He reviled, counted and called a blasphemer, a wine bibber, a Samaritan, a devil! How was He stoned, thrust out of the synogogues, arraigned a deceiver of the people, a seditious and pestilent fellow, an enemy of Caesar and as such scourged, spit upon, condemned and nailed to an accursed tree!

C. Because the Saints of All Ages Experience It.

How soon was Abel made a martyr for his religion and Isaac mocked by the son of the bond woman! Read the Acts of the Apostles and see how the Christians were threatened, stoned, imprisoned, scourged, and martyred! Examine church history in after ages and the experiences of saints now living and I am persuaded that everyone will concur with the Apostles' statement, that "all who will live godly in Christ Jesus, shall suffer persecution."

D. Because of the Sinners' Enmity Against God.

Wicked men hate God and therefore cannot but hate those who are like Him. They hate to be reformed and therefore they must hate and persecute those who by a contrary behavior testify against them that their lives are evil. Pride of heart leads men to persecute Christ's servants. They dare not imitate, therefore they persecute. Christians are not of the world, but Christ has chosen them out of the world, therefore the world hates them.

E. Because the Godly Need It.

If we have not all manner of evil spoken of us, how can we know whether we love contempt and seek only that honor which come from above? If we have not persecution, how can our passive graces be kept in exercise? How can many Christian precepts be put into practice? How can we love, pray for, and do good to those who despitefully use us? How can we overcome evil with good? How can we love God better than life itself?

CONCLUSION

Not all are persecuted in a like degree, yet all Christians will find by their own experience that whether they act in a private or public capacity they must in some degree or other suffer persecution.

Not all who are persecuted are real Christians; for many sometimes suffer and are persecuted on other accounts than for righteousness' sake. The great question is, whether you are ever persecuted for living godly. If not, let the text sound an alarm in your ears and sink deep into your hearts.

34

Soul Prosperity

Beloved, I wish above all things that thou mayest prosper, and be in health, even as thy soul prospereth. **—III John 2**

I AM SURE that there are some that if it were put to their choice had rather know that their soul prospers than to have fifty thousand dollars bequeathed to them. The great question is how shall I know that my soul prospers. Therefore, it will not be unprofitable to lay down some marks whereby we may know whether our souls are prospering or not.

I. PRAYER IS A MARK OF SOUL PROSPERITY.

A. Its Necessity.

1. *The testimony of godly men.* John Bunyan said, if we are prayerless, we are Christless. None of God's people come into the world still-born. The commentator Burket agrees: "Come into the world still-born! What language is that in a preacher's mouth?"

2. *The testimony of Scripture.* "I will pour out a Spirit of grace and supplication," says the Lord; and I will venture to say, if the Spirit of grace resides in the heart, the Spirit of supplication will not be wanting.

B. Its Nature.

1. *It is voluntary.* Persons under their first love dare not go without God; they go to God, not as the formalist does, not for fear of going to hell or being condemned. A person

that has just been brought to a liberty of the sons of God goes freely to his heavenly Father.

2. *It is constrained by love.* Did not you hearken unto God like a fond mother if her beloved child made but the least noise? You could no more keep from the presence of God than the loving mother from the presence of her dear child. If your soul prospers, this connection between you and God will be kept up.

C. Its Outcome.

1. *Faithfulness to the means of grace.* If our souls prosper we will conscientiously attend on the means of grace. It is a most dreadful mark when persons think they are so high in grace that they thank God that they have no need of them. The various means of grace are intended for the nourishing of all God's children.

2. *Love for the messengers of grace.* If our soul prospers we shall be glad for a good plain country dish, as well as a fine garnished desert. If our souls prosper we shall be fond of the messengers as well as the message. We shall admire as much to hear a good ram's horn as a fine silver trumpet.

II. A GROWING KNOWLEDGE OF ONESELF IS A MARK OF SOUL PROSPERITY.

A. It Makes One More Sensible of His State.

1. *His outward state.* The knowledge of ourselves is the first thing God implants. "Lord let me know myself," was a prayer which one of the Church Fathers prayed. If you have high thoughts of yourselves you forget what poor silly creatures you are. Our first battle is with the outward man.

2. *His inward state.* As our souls prosper we shall be more and more sensible, not only of the outside, but of the inside. As we advance in the Christian life we have nearer views of the chambers of imagery that are in our hearts;

and one day after another we find more and more abomination there.

B. It Makes One More Sensible of Christ's Glory.

1. *The glory of the One who is our deliverer.* Day by day we see more of the glory of Jesus Christ, the wonders of that Immanuel who daily delivers us from this body of sin and death.

2. *The glory of the One who is our righteousness.* I never knew a person in my life that diligently used the Bible and other means but as they improved in grace saw more and more of the necessity of depending upon a better righteousness than their own. If we grow in grace the Spirit of God leads us out of self and causes us to flee more and more to that glorious and complete righteousness that Jesus Christ wrought out.

C. It Makes One More Sensible to God's Grace.

The more your souls prosper, the more you will see of the freeness and distinguishing nature of God's grace, that all is of grace. We all naturally depend on ourselves. Therefore young Christians often say, "We have found the Messiah," whereas later, the believer learns that the Messiah had found him.

III. A VICTORIOUS LIFE IS A MARK OF SOUL PROSPERITY.

A. This Includes Good Works.

1. *Good works do not constitute a basis for salvation.* Perhaps some stranger will say, "I thought you were against good works." I tell you the truth, I am against good works; but do not run away before I finish my sentence; I am against good works being put in the room of Christ as the ground of our acceptance.

2. *Good works are the result of salvation.* An idle person tempts the devil to tempt him. In the state of paradise, Adam and Eve were to dress the garden and not to be idle

there. After the fall they were to till the ground. A Christian should work hard that he may have to give to them who are in need.

B. This Includes a Growing Love.

1. *The failure to love.* There are some good souls, but very narrow souls, who are afraid of loving people who differ from them. Party spirits creep in among Christians. Whereas it was formerly said, "See how these Christians love one another!" now it may be said, "See how these Christians hate one another." People may boast of their wild-fire zeal for God, until they cannot bear the sight of a person who differs from them.

2. *The commendation of love.* The Apostle commands Gaius for his love. That was a glorious saying of a good Scottish woman, "Come in, ye blessed of the Lord, I have a house that will hold a hundred and a heart that will hold ten thousand." God give us such a heart. "He that dwelleth in love, dwelleth in God."

CONCLUSION

When I think of what God has done for me and how little I have done for Him, it makes me weep and cry, "Oh, my leanness." This makes me long to be in earnest for my Lord. What do you say? Have all of you the same desire?

35

A Faithful Minister's Parting Blessing

> *The grace of our Lord Jesus Christ be with you all. Amen.*
>
> — **Revelation 22:21**

I$_T$ $_{IS}$ very remarkable that the Old Testament ends with the word curse, whereby we are taught that the law made nothing perfect; but the New Testament ends otherwise, even with a precious blessing, that glorious grace put into the heart and dropped by the pen of the disciple whom Jesus loved. I can wish nothing better than that the words of our text may be fulfilled in our hearts.

I. THE INTERPRETATION OF GRACE.

A. It Is in General God's Favor to the World.

Perhaps there is not a word in the Bible that has a greater variety of interpretations than the word *grace*. I do not intend to give you all of them. It will be enough in general to observe that the word signifies favor or may imply the general kindness that God bears to the world.

B. It Is Specifically the Work of the Holy Spirit in the Lives of God's People.

It signifies here the special grace of God communicated to His people; not only His favor displayed to us outwardly, but the work of God's Spirit imparted and conveyed inwardly and most powerfully to our souls. Grace takes in all that the Spirit of God does for a sinner from the moment he first draws his breath and brings him to Jesus Christ until He is pleased to call him by death.

II. THE DESCRIPTION OF GRACE.

A. It Is the Grace of Jesus Christ Because He Procured It.

It is called "the grace of our Lord Jesus Christ" because He purchased it for us. If the Lord Jesus had not bought us with a price, even the price of His own blood, you and I would never have the grace of God manifested to our souls.

B. It Is the Grace of Jesus Christ Because He Conveys It.

Moreover, this grace may be called "the grace of our Lord Jesus Christ" because it is conveyed into our hearts through Him. The Federal Head of His glorious body is a head of influence to those for whom He shed His blood. Thus His disciples said He was full of grace and truth and out of His fulness we receive grace upon grace.

III. THE CLASSIFICATION OF GRACE.

A. Restraining Grace.

If it were not for restraining grace God's people would be just as weak and wicked as other folks. The Son of God is always acting in a restraining way to His people; if it were not so, by the blindness of their understandings, the corruptions of their hearts and affections, together with the perverseness of their will; there is not a Christian that would not run away every day if Christ did not restrain him.

B. Convicting Grace.

There is convicting grace which acts every day and hour. It is a blessed thing to be under the Redeemer's convicting grace. I am not speaking of convicting grace that wounds before conversion and gives us a sense of sin and misery; I mean convicting grace that follows the believer from time to time.

C. Converting Grace.

We can no more turn our hearts than we can turn the world upside down. (1) It is the Redeemer by His Spirit that takes away the heart of stone and gives us a heart of flesh. (2) In the divine life, not to go forward is to go backward and it is one part of the work of the Holy Spirit to convert the soul from something that is wrong to something that is right.

D. Establishing Grace.

Many people have some religion, but they are not established; hence they are mere weather vanes turned about by every wind of doctrine. As believers grow in grace and in the knowledge of Christ they will be more settled, more confirmed, more manly, more firm, more steady.

E. Comforting Grace.

"In the multitude of my thoughts within me," says the Psalmist, "Thy comforts have refreshed my soul" (Psalm 94:19). We shall never be content or cheerful under sufferings but through the assistance of the Redeemer. In respect of parting from one another, what can comfort friends when separated but the Spirit of God? There are so many afflictions and trials that if it were not for the Lord Jesus Christ's comfortings no flesh could bear them.

F. Quickening Grace.

"The winter is past, the rain is over and gone, the flowers appear on the earth, the time of the singing of birds is come and the voice of the turtle is heard in our land, the fig tree putteth forth her green figs, and the vines with the tender grapes give a good smell" (Song of Solomon 2:12). What is all this but God's quickening grace, restoring the believer to his blessed joy?

IV. THE MINISTRATIONS OF GRACE.

A. In Prayer.

The grace of our Lord Jesus Christ is with His people in prayer. Who can pray without grace?

B. In Bible Reading.

What profit will it be to us to read the Scriptures without the grace of God? Jesus Christ must open our minds to understand the Word of God, and the Spirit of God must take the things of Christ and show them to us.

C. In Providence.

The people of God see Him in His providence; the very hairs of their heads are all numbered and the grace of God is with them in every affair of life.

D. In Everyday Life.

The grace of God is with His people in the common business of life. We preach that the grace of God may attend men in their businesses and professions, and woe be to those persons who do not take the grace of God with them.

E. In Sickness and Death.

The grace of our Lord Jesus Christ is with His people when sick and dying. O my dear souls, what shall we do when death comes? What a mercy it is that we have a good Master to take us through that time. As another has said, "Do not fear, Jesus Christ will carry you safely through the dark valley of the shadow of death."

CONCLUSION

May the grace of God be with every unconverted soul. What will you do with the favor of man if you have not the grace of God? If you have the grace of God the Lord grant you more grace. Grace, mercy, and peace be multiplied to all of you.